Employment and Dyslexia Handbook 2009

Edited by **Dr Ian Smythe**

Published by

The British Dyslexia Association

Unit 8 Bracknell Beeches, Old Bracknell Lane, Bracknell, RG12 7BW

Helpline: 0845 251 9002
Administration: 0845 251 9003
Website: www.bdadyslexia.org.uk

ISBN 978-1-872653-97-6
Price: £10.00

The British Dyslexia Association

President
Baroness Warnock of Weeke

Chair
Margaret Malpas

Vice Presidents
Lord Addington
Diana Baring
Professor Angela Fawcett
Lady Jane Lloyd
Sir Nick Monck KCB
Kevin Morley
Professor Peter Pumphrey CPsychol FBPsS
The Lord Renwick
Ian Smith
Professor Margaret Snowling
Sir Jackie Stewart OBE
Anne Watts CBE

The British Dyslexia Association aims to ensure that there is a way forward for every dyslexic person, so that he or she receives appropriate teaching, help and support, and is given an equal opportunity to achieve his or her potential in order to lead a fulfilled and happy life.

Employment and Dyslexia Handbook 2009

A compendium of articles and resources for dyslexic people, their families, fellow workers, managers, and supervisors.

Edited by **Dr Ian Smythe**

Published by
British Dyslexia Association

Editorial Note

The views expressed in this book are those of the individual contributors, and do not necessarily represent the policy of the British Dyslexia Association.

The BDA does not endorse the advertisements included in this publication.

Whilst every effort has been made to ensure the accuracy of information given in this handbook, the BDA cannot accept responsibility for the consequences of any errors or omissions in that information.

In certain articles the masculine pronoun is used purely for the sake of convenience.

British Dyslexia Association

The Dyslexia Handbook 2009
1. Great Britain. Education
2. Title 11. Dr Ian Smythe
3. ISBN 978-1-872653-97-6

Published in Great Britain 2009 © Copyright British Dyslexia Association 2009

Printed by   PPG Print, Portsmouth, Hampshire
             www.ppgprint.co.uk

Advertising sales by Space Marketing
Tel: 01892 677740
Fax: 01892 677743
Email: brians@spacemarketing.co.uk

British Dyslexia Association
Unit 8, Bracknell Beeches, Old Bracknell Lane, Bracknell RG12 7BW
Helpline: 0845 251 9002
Administration: 0845 251 9003
Fax: 0845 251 9005

Website: www.bdadyslexia.org.uk

BDA is a company limited by guarantee, registered in England No. 1830587
Registered Charity No. 289243

Contents

1. Understanding Dyslexia   1

1.1 About the BDA   1
Judi Stewart

1.2 What is Dyslexia?   5
Kate Saunders

1.3 Checklist for Adults with Dyslexia   15
Ian Smythe and John Everatt

**1.4 Overlap of Specific Learning Difficulties
and Dyslexia**   18
Amanda Kirby

1.5 Case Study - *Arran Smith*   25

1.6 Forces for Change in the Workplace   26
Margaret Malpas

**1.7 A Snapshot of Dyslexia from a
Research Perspective**   31
Joel B. Talcott

1.8 Research in Adults with Dyslexia   40
John Everatt

1.9 Dyslexia in the Workplace in Wales   46
Welsh Dyslexia Project

1.10 Case Study - *Edward Charvet*   50

1.11 A European Policy Perspective   52
European Dyslexia Association

1.12 Giving hope in the USA   57
Glenn Young

2. Assessing Strengths and Weaknesses 63

2.1 The Assessment of Dyslexic Adults 63
David McLoughlin

2.2 Identifying Skills for Careers and the Workplace 69
Sue Flohr

2.3 Case Study - Chris Fortey 75

2.4 Maths in the Workplace 76
Steve Chinn

2.5 Perfect for Business - School Failure, Work Success 82
Thomas G. West

2.6 Workplace needs Assessments: How to Arrange and Appraise them 86
Sylvia Moody

2.7 Case Study - Professor Paul Palmer 94

3. Using Technology 96

3.1 What's hot in technology? 96
Ian Smythe

3.2 Network Solutions 99
Dave Evans

3.3 Using Text to Speech to Support Reading and Writing in the Workplace 104
Sally McKeown and Dave Stevens

3.4 Case Study- Jason Crandley 109

3.5 Assistive Technology for the Workplace 111
EA Draffan

3.6 AdysTrain - Supporting Dyslexics in the European Workforce 117
Bernadette Frech and Thomas Schmalzer

3.7 Towards a Corporate Policy on Accessible Format Materials 120
Ian Litterick

3.8 Case Study - Cara Cramp 127

3.9 Speech-to-text: Putting Together the Right Solution 129
Peter Kelway

4. Dyslexia Friendly Working Practices 135

4.1 Accessible Websites 135
Graeme Whippy

4.2 Shared Responsibility 146
Judi Stewart

4.3 Case Study - *Mike Poole* 151

4.4 Creativity - Harnessing Talent 153
Kevin Morley

4.5 Coping Strategies 157
Lord Addington

4.6 Designing Dyslexia Friendly Reading Materials 160
Patience Thomson

5. Supporting Dyslexic Individuals 165

5.1 Dyslexia and Unemployment 165
Alan Shoreman

5.2 Case Study - *Ki McRoberts* 170

5.3 Working with Dyslexia in the Healthcare and 172
Emergency Services
Carol Leather

5.4 Appreciating and Making the Most of Strengths 178
Bonita Thomson

5.5 Identifying Skills for Work and Career Guidance 184
Steve O'Brien

5.6 Supporting Dyslexic Employees 191
Ellen Morgan

5.7 Case Study - *Vicki McNicol* 197

5.8 Raising Self-Esteem 199
Vicki Godwin

5.9 Dyslexia: the Line Manager's Challenge 204
Katherine Kindersley

5.10 Towards Inclusive Practice in the Workplace 213
Nicky Martin

5.11 Dyslexia: Should Managers be Knowledgeable? 220
Anne Kent

6. Into Employment 226

**6.1 Dyslexia Career Strategies and matching 226
Competencies with Job Requirements**
Brian Hagan

6.2 How SKIDZ supports the Dyslexic Individual 235
Steve Godfrey

6.3 Dyslexia in the Workplace: the Legal Requirements 239
John Mackenzie

6.4 Case Study - Peter Hall 245

6.5 Legal Remedies 247
Melanie Jameson

6.6 Preparing Students for Employment 254
Barry Hayward

6.7 Retailing and Dyslexia 260
Trevor Hobbs

Index of Advertisers 266

Editor's Foreword

When Judi Stewart, Chief Executive of the British Dyslexia Association, first asked me to edit this new Handbook, I had nightmares from the last time I did a BDA Handbook in 2001. The hours of sweat and tears, the contributors missing deadlines, and problems with .... almost everything. But I have to admit this has been a sheer delight.

Furthermore, seventeen of the forty plus articles are written by dyslexics. And the dyslexics were the ones to send their contributions first. Could this be a sign of a coping strategy working well?

Please note that we have tried not to "over-edit" the text, to allow each contributor to express themselves appropriately, and promote a diversity of styles.

On the layout itself, the BDA tries hard to ensure and promote dyslexia-friendly approaches. This includes using clear typefaces, clear layout, and set in a way that is readable to most text to speech engines. Hence, for example, full stops at the end of headers and in abbreviations.

Ian Smythe

1. Understanding Dyslexia

1.1 About the BDA

Judi Stewart, Chief Executive, British Dyslexia Association

About the BDA

The British Dyslexia Association (BDA) is the national organisation for specific learning difficulties and represents over two million children and adults with dyslexia. It was formed in 1972 to support the development of Local Dyslexia Associations across the UK. It currently has 85 Local Dyslexia Associations, as well as Organisational and Individual members. The BDA works in conjunction with the Local Dyslexia Associations, acting on the issues that affect people at the national level and providing a National Helpline that receives approximately 20,000 calls a year and over 4,500 emails a year. The Local Dyslexia Associations play a dual role by providing support focused on individuals, their homes and places of work or education as well as collecting valuable data on the issues that really concern people. Some of the Local Associations have support groups especially for adults and many provide a Helpline. Such services are listed at the end of this article.

A key asset of the BDA is the fact that it supports dyslexic people of any age, from pre-education, through education and into employment. Transition points are particularly difficult for dyslexic people and a holistic overview of how one system links to the others is important. The BDA is also fortunate to have a system that works at the national and local level, with much of the work being carried out by volunteers. The combination of professional knowledge alongside those who have known and experienced the pains and the joys works well. There is a good balance between support and the reality that, in the end, effort is required to 'master' dyslexia and allow individuals' talents to shine through. The BDA wants to make sure that support is always at hand, providing opportunities to learn, work and play from age 1 to 101.

The BDA's vision - "A dyslexia friendly society enabling all dyslexic people to reach their potential" - is based on creating change at a fundamental level that is firmly embedded in society. Progress has already been made, with dyslexia already identified as a disability in the Disability Discrimination Act 2005, but in many respects the culture change is only beginning. Dyslexia affects 10% of the British population, with 4% of this group believed to be severely dyslexic. This is a large group of people which should mean that the needs of dyslexic people are recognised in every educational establishment and any workplace. In fact this is not the case. Many dyslexic people across the UK are unable to fulfil their potential as most of the population still do not understand what dyslexia is, the difficulties which dyslexic people have and how best to support them. Dyslexia is not an obvious difficulty, it is hidden. As a result, dyslexic people have to overcome numerous barriers to make a full contribution to society.

Disappointingly there is still a large group of dyslexic people leaving school with few or no qualifications. 30%-50 % of those in the criminal justice system are dyslexic and many others cannot find employment or a means to address their learning difficulties. This creates an enormous barrier as well as a great deal of frustration and anger. Those caught in this negative cycle find they not only have to cope with their dyslexia but also have no access to education and, in most cases, have very low self-esteem. After many years of failing and in most cases being told they are 'thick' or 'stupid' they have no means to live as independent adults. This is an intolerable position and a key area of policy and campaign work for the BDA. Much of the campaigning work needs to focus on changes in the school system but there is also a need to help those who have not been able to access an adequate education, or still have significant problems in managing their dyslexia, and to create or change the systems that support this adult group.

Last year the BDA launched an Employability Campaign to address a wide range of these issues. At the same time as creating change through policy, campaigning and setting standards, there is a need to support and enable people directly. It is easy to say to an employer that they must abide by the Disability Discrimination Act (and so they must) but a real cultural change requires the recognition that dyslexic people can and do make positive contributions. Recently, research has begun to demonstrate what many have recognised for years, that dyslexic people tend to be lateral thinkers and creative in the broadest sense of the word. For some time a group of successful dyslexic people have been recognized, people such as Richard Branson (Virgin Group), Guy Hands (Terra Firma) and Sir Phil Harris (Carpetright plc) but they tended to be seen as the 'lucky ones'. However, research such as that conducted by Cass Business School is beginning to demonstrate that there is a much larger group of successful dyslexic people. Cass found that "Dyslexics make up 19% or 600,000 of the 3.5 million entrepreneurial population in the U.K." compared with a 10% general incidence of dyslexia. The BDA is not alone in thinking that further research will provide more such evidence and that improvements in the education system and workplace will allow more dyslexic people to demonstrate their talents.

The BDA also provides an on-going programme of support and advice. Directors, managers and colleagues all need to have a general awareness of dyslexia so that support can be managed as an everyday event. To achieve this, the BDA runs a training programme as well as conferences across the country. Information about these events can be found on the BDA website, which also has a great many facts and tips to support the employer, employee and those wanting help to find work. The BDA website has an on-line shop that sells the latest assistive technology and other products to support dyslexic people. The choice can seem a little daunting but the National Helpline will guide an individual as to what might suit them. The BDA will not endorse products but there is certainly recognition that assistive technology is part of the solution for dyslexic people and the Association works hard to make sure there is a good range of high quality and affordable options available.

Embedding standards is part of the long-term solution. This covers both educational establishments and the workplace. The BDA's Quality Mark is a verification system that, once awarded, can demonstrate to the world that an organisation has reached the minimum standards. This directly affects both staff and customers. The more organisations that have the BDA Quality Mark the more dyslexia friendly and dyslexia tolerant society becomes.

The BDA is about creating change, setting standards and supporting people. Our most important job is to enable dyslexic people to reach their potential and each year there is more to celebrate as the barriers to dyslexic people begin to crumble.

1.2 What is Dyslexia?

Kate Saunders, Education and Policy Director,
British Dyslexia Association

Dyslexia is a specific learning difficulty that mainly affects
the development of literacy and language related skills. It is
likely to be present at birth and to be life-long in its effects. It
is characterised by difficulties with phonological processing,
rapid naming, working memory, processing speed, and the
automatic development of skills that may not match up to an
individual's other cognitive abilities. It tends to be resistant to
conventional teaching methods, but its effects can be mitigated
by appropriately specific intervention, including the application
of information technology and supportive counselling.

This is the definition of dyslexia approved by the Management
Board of the British Dyslexia Association (BDA) (2007).

Specific Learning Difficulties (SpLD) is an umbrella term that
covers a number of difficulties, including dyslexia, dyscalculia,
dyspraxia, attention deficit disorders and Asperger's syndrome.
Some of these difficulties have certain shared characteristics
and there can be co-morbidity (i.e. some dyslexics can
sometimes also show another SpLD).

Dyslexic individuals generally show an uneven profile of
cognitive scores, with relative strengths and specific weaknesses
in certain areas (hence specific learning difficulty). The
relative strengths shown by dyslexics can include the areas of
vocabulary and non-verbal problem-solving ability. For many
dyslexics their general verbal skills may also be relatively
good. It is widely agreed that dyslexic individuals generally
experience difficulties with phonological processing. They can

have difficulty linking letter shapes to letter sounds, difficulty breaking words down into sound units, difficulty constructing words for spelling from sound units and difficulty building up an awareness of the way that sounds work within words (e.g. being able to separate the first or final sounds within words). Word retrieval and speed of processing can also be affected.

It has been suggested that differences in the functioning of the cerebellum may contribute to dyslexics finding it difficult to establish automaticity in key areas (e.g. within reading and spelling skills). There can be persisting left-right confusions. There may also be associated difficulties with grapho-motor skills (affecting the smooth movement of the pen across the page) and visuo-motor perceptual skills (which can create difficulties with letter formation and spacing on the page).

These difficulties can hamper the early acquisition of written language skills (reading, writing and spelling) and may also have a negative effect when working with musical notation. There is an associated difficulty with mathematics, referred to as 'dyscalculia'. This can occur independently of dyslexia, or it can sometimes occur with dyslexia in the same individual. However, in general dyslexics often have relatively good mathematical skills, but they may show difficulties with certain aspects of number work (e.g. remembering strings of numbers and equations, learning times tables by rote and where there are visuo-motor perceptual difficulties, sometimes difficulty remembering, accurately reproducing and 'setting out' complex patterns of working for set operations).

Difficulties with working memory are often evident. These are generally tested by the assessor saying strings of numbers of increasing length, which the individual has to say back, initially in the same order, but in the second part of the test in reverse order. A severe dyslexic might have (amongst other signs) difficulty consistently correctly repeating back in reverse order as few as two numbers. This difficulty with working memory can be reflected in difficulty remembering a string of instructions or numbers (e.g. learning times tables by rote, remembering pin numbers, taking telephone messages accurately). It also has implications for areas such as organisational skills, where the individual may reach 'overload' if they have too many tasks to hold in their working memory at once. A strategy that is useful to help overcome this is for the individual to break the list of tasks down into 'chunks' of two, do those two things, then focus on the next two, rather than trying to remember in their head a long string of things to do.

Of course, aids such as lists, organisers, secretaries and technology can also help. In general, the effects of dyslexia can be mitigated by aspects in the environment around the individual. For example, the use of assistive technology can be very helpful and this has developed tremendously in the last few years. 'Read text' programmes will read out loud what is on the screen and that can include text that has been scanned in, arrived by e-mail or viewed on the internet. Speech recognition tools have also become more accurate and user friendly.

Research indicates that there are differences in aspects of brain structure in dyslexics and non-dyslexics. Magnetic Resonance Imaging (MRI) has also demonstrated that different areas of the brain are activated when dyslexics and non-dyslexics are engaged in reading tasks. For dyslexics there also appear to be some difficulties with the processing of rapidly moving visual stimuli (as occurs in the magnocellular visual system when reading) and also possibly with aspects of auditory processing (at magnocellular level).

Dyslexics can experience visual stress symptoms when reading, where it is suggested that sensitivity to the glare effect on the white page can lead to effects such as blurring of print. (Coloured acetate sheets, tinted lenses and pale coloured paper can all help to reduce this effect.) Dyslexics may also experience difficulty with visual tracking skills (i.e. their eyes may 'jump' more than non-dyslexics when they read along a line of print) and visual convergence difficulties. This concerns the way that the two eyes work to focus together on a particular point (e.g. where the print is on the page). Eye exercises and sometimes prescribed glasses may help with these aspects, following assessment from an optometrist.

Dyslexia tends to run in families. One or both parents may have dyslexic difficulties, or someone in the wider family may have these difficulties (although they may not have been formally diagnosed). There is growing (although not always consistent) evidence possibly linking a tendency towards dyslexia with gene markers on certain chromosomes (e.g. chromosomes 1, 2, 3, 6, 15, 18). It seems probable that there will be a complex biological picture with several factors combining to produce an individual who is susceptible to dyslexia. Research has suggested that for a male dyslexic, there may be around a 40% chance of having a dyslexic son and around an 18% chance of having a dyslexic daughter. For a dyslexic woman there may be around a 35% chance of having a dyslexic son and an 18% chance of having a dyslexic daughter.

It is appropriate, therefore, for adult dyslexics and those who have dyslexia within the wider family, to be aware of the early indications of a possible dyslexic difficulty. 'At risk' signs may be evident from as young as 3 years of age and certainly up to 5 or 6 years of age children should be carefully monitored for possible signs. These might include some delay in the acquisition of speech, glue-ear and intermittent hearing loss, difficulties with aspects of fine and gross motor co-ordination, difficulty with sound discrimination and speech articulation, difficulty copying and forming letters, sequencing, linking letter sounds and symbols, breaking words down into individual sounds (phonemes) and being aware of the way that sounds work within words (e.g. rhyming).

These children may very much enjoy listening to stories that are read to them, but not be as keen as their peers to engage with the task of reading themselves. Often the experienced teacher will feel that the child is showing more difficulty with the acquisition of pre-literacy and early literacy skills than they would have expected for the child's apparent ability in oral communication and problem-solving, construction and creative ability. Vigilance from parents, teachers and schools (who should ideally have screening methods in place or at least available, although this is not common enough practice currently) at this early stage can lead to early identification and intervention, which provides the best long-term prognosis.

The effects of dyslexia on reading, writing and spelling skills can be reduced through early identification and the provision of a well structured, multi-sensory phonics based teaching programme, coupled with explicit teaching of spelling rules and patterns. These enable the dyslexic to work out how to read and spell words when they cannot automatically recall how to do so. The past decade has seen encouraging improvements in the use of structured phonics based programmes and multi-sensory learning methods in classroom teaching in the early few years of schooling. There continue to be children, however, who need targeted intervention programmes (both small group and one to one) to boost their phonological and literacy skills, as they need more reinforcement and consolidation than is possible within the pace of the curriculum. These intervention programmes should be planned and ideally delivered by specialist SpLD/dyslexia trained teachers, who can also carry out detailed assessments of the profile and needs of the individual child and focus the programme appropriately. The BDA is working with other dyslexia organisations to campaign for one dyslexia specialist trained teacher in every school.

Experience and research would indicate that where sufficient levels of such targeted intervention is given (in terms of the number of sessions a week and the length of the programme), dyslexic children generally do not have to show marked difficulty with literacy skills that persist into adulthood. Tragically, of course, for many adults sufficient levels of appropriate specialist teaching were not available to them when younger and for some dyslexics the persisting impairment in literacy skills has a very serious impact on their adult lives, limiting their career choices and providing obstacles in daily living.

Adult dyslexics can often have low self-esteem and low-confidence. They may feel vulnerable and disadvantaged due to persisting difficulties with literacy, working memory, time management and organisational skills. They may try to compensate through extra effort and time input at work but this can lead them to excessive fatigue. Stress levels can be high and the signs of dyslexia can become more prominent when the individual is under stress. This in turn can exacerbate anxiety levels.

In some cases, frustration, anger and restricted opportunities can give rise to other secondary emotional and behavioural difficulties. It has been a fairly consistent research finding for many years that there are a disproportionate number of dyslexic individuals in prisons.

On the positive side, there are also a disproportionate number of dyslexics among successful entrepreneurs. Dyslexics can show strengths in certain areas. These may include visual thinking, creativity, divergent thinking, three dimensional thinking, 'gestalt' thinking (being able to see the 'overview'), picture memory and 'video' memory. This is where the individual makes a kind of 'video' in their mind of what they see before them. This memory may include colour, sound, sequence of events and 'locus' (place). Other areas of strength may include understanding and remembering stories and meaning, motor and tactile memory, construction skills, logic, empathy, pattern recognition and sometimes good memory for mnemonics, tunes and rhythm. Dyslexics can show great energy, curiosity and concentration (although generally not for written language tasks) for topics that interest them.

Those adult dyslexics who have been able largely to overcome their difficulties may also show good problem solving skills, determination and perseverance. Some individuals regard their own dyslexia as a 'gift'.

The BDA encourages companies and organisations to adopt Dyslexia Friendly working practices and will guide them in working towards the BDA dyslexia friendly Quality Mark award. This includes practical components but also involves the company showing an understanding of the difficulties faced by dyslexic individuals and supporting them in order to maximise their potential and performance levels, without undue stress and anxiety. On an individual level, BDA assessors can evaluate and make recommendations about the needs of an individual within the workplace and how the individual and the company can maximise the individual's effectiveness.

There are some myths about dyslexia:

1. *"It is a middle class excuse".*
   False. Dyslexia occurs across all social categories. Being dyslexic means that the individual has to work harder to achieve their goals, not less hard.

2. *"All dyslexics reverse their b's and d's."*
   False. The majority of very young children will sometimes reverse letters in the early years of schooling. Some dyslexics continue to reverse b's and d's beyond the developmental age when most young children will have stopped doing so. However, this is not universal among dyslexics and it is certainly possible for an individual to be dyslexic and not do this. Difficulty with aspects of phonological skills is a more common sign of dyslexia.

3. *"A person can't be dyslexic if they can read."*
   False. Dyslexic individuals do generally experience difficulty with the early acquisition of literacy skills. However, some adult dyslexics will have been able to develop good functional reading skills. This is particularly likely if they have received appropriate teaching and support. However, quite often in such cases, the dyslexic individual may have effective decoding skills but reading speed may be slower than their peers and they may find reading quite hard work. The number of books they read in a year may tend to be comparatively low and adult dyslexics will often report that they tend to read for information, not pleasure (although some will do so and dyslexics can have great appreciation for the language and content of good literature). Spelling can be a more persistent difficulty (although again good teaching can be effective in establishing good skills). At Further Education, Higher Education and adult level, there

are many well compensated dyslexics whose persisting difficulties lie in the areas of higher order study and organisational skills (e.g. organising large pieces of written work, summarising, note-taking, time management, speed of processing of auditory information, and effective revision and examination techniques). Dyslexia is a complex pattern of difficulties affecting a number of different areas, not just reading. Individual dyslexics show different elements out of this 'cluster' of difficulties.

In summary, there are biological and cognitive aspects underpinning dyslexia. Elements within the environment of the individual also contribute towards the impact these factors may have on the individual and their lives. There are some variations in definitions of dyslexia within the field and there is some persisting lack of consensus. Dyslexic adults should be supported to understand the nature of their difficulties and potential strengths. The key aim of the BDA is to work to bring about a Dyslexia Friendly Society.

References:

Elliot, E. (2008) Back to the Sky. How to Fly with Dyslexia. Olympia Publishers, London.

Fawcett, A J. (Ed.) (2001) Dyslexia: Theory and Good Practice. Whurr Publishers, London.

Hulme, C. & Snowling, M, (1997) Dyslexia: Biology, Cognition and Intervention. Whurr Publishers Ltd, London.

McLoughlin, D et al, (1994) Adult Dyslexia: Assessment, Counselling and Training. Whurr Publishers Ltd.

Reid R. and Wearmouth J. (2002) Dyslexia and Literacy: Theory and Practice. John Wiley & Sons Ltd.

Saunders, K. and White, A (2002) How Dyslexics Learn: Grasping the Nettle. PATOSS, Evesham.

T.R. Miles (Ed) (2004) Dyslexia and Stress. Whurr publishers, London

Vogler, G.P., DeFries, J.C & Decker, S.N. (1985) Family history as an indicator of risk of reading disability. Journal of Learning Disabilities, 18: 491-421

1.3 Checklist for Adults with Dyslexia

Ian Smythe and John Everatt

There are many ways in which a checklist for dyslexic adults may be used. Whilst it will not provide enough information for a diagnostic assessment it can be very useful in providing a better self-understanding and be a pointer towards future assessment needs.

Here, Ian Smythe and John Everatt explain their work. In an attempt to overcome the difficulties of previous checklists (eg. the use of 'yes' and 'no' as possible answers), over the past few years we have been piloting and testing a new checklist for dyslexic adults which is set out here. The results are based on extensive questioning in many contexts and not just within the traditional area of higher education. The results have provided a valuable insight into the diversity of difficulties and is a clear reminder that every individual is different and should be treated and assessed as such. However, it is also interesting to note that a number of questions, the answers to which are said to be characteristics of dyslexic adults, are commonly found in the answers of non-dyslexics.

On the following pages are the questions that were found to be more predictive of dyslexia (as measured by prior diagnosis). In order to provide what we consider to be the most informative checklist we have used scores for each answer which indicate the relative importance of that questions. Alongside each line you can keep a tally of which you score and in the end find a total.

For each question circle the box which is closest to your response, from 'rarely' to 'most of the time'. For example, if you frequently have trouble filling in forms, put a circle around 3 (the number in the 'frequently' column) and write the number in the total column.

	Rarely	Occasionally	Often	Most of the Time
1. Do you confuse visually similar words such as cat and cot?	3	6	9	12
2. Do you lose your place or miss out lines when reading?	2	4	6	8
3. Do you confuse the names of objects, for example table for chair?	1	2	4	4
4. Do you have trouble telling left from right?	1	2	4	4
5. Is map reading or finding your way to a strange place confusing?	1	2	4	4
6. Do you re-read paragraphs to understand them?	1	2	4	4
7. Do you get confused when given several instructions at once?	1	2	4	4
8. Do you make mistakes when taking down telephone messages?	1	2	4	4
9. Do you find it difficult to find the right word to say?	1	2	4	4
10. How often do you think of creative solutions to problems?	1	2	4	4
	Easy	Challenging	Difficult	Very Difficult
11. How easy do you find it to sound out words such as e-le-phant?	3	6	9	12
12. When writing, do you find it difficult to organise thoughts on paper?	2	4	6	8
13. Did you learn your multiplication tables easily?	2	4	6	8
14. How easy do you find it to recite the alphabet?	1	2	3	4
15. How hard do you find it to read aloud?	1	2	3	4

Results from the Adults Test - what it all means

It is important to remember that this does not constitute an assessment of one's difficulties. It is just an indication of some of the areas in which you or the person you are assessing may have difficulties. It is important to stress that only through an extensive assessment, carried out by those who have a real understanding of the potential difficulties, can a full understanding of difficulties be reached. However this questionnaire may provide a better awareness of the nature of the difficulties. If you use this questionnaire it should be for personal interest and should not be used to decide whether to seek further support.

Whilst we do stress that this is not a diagnostic tool, we can state that our research suggests the following:

Score less than 45 - probably non-dyslexic
Research results: no individual who was diagnosed as dyslexic through a full assessment was found to have scored less than 45 and therefore it is unlikely that if you score under 45 you will be dyslexic.

Score 45 to 60 - showing signs consistent with mild dyslexia
Research results: most of those who were in this category showed signs of being at least moderately dyslexic. However, a number of persons not diagnosed as dyslexic (though they could just be unrecognised and undiagnosed) all fell into this category.

Score Greater than 60 - signs consistent with moderate or severe dyslexia.

Research results: all those who recorded of scores of more than 60 were diagnosed as moderately or severely dyslexic. Therefore we would suggest that a score greater than 60 suggests moderate or severe dyslexia.

Please note that this should not be regarded as an assessment of one's difficulties. But if you feel that a dyslexia-type problem may exist, further advice should be sought. Your local dyslexia association may also be able to help. The BDA helpline number is 0845 251 9002.

1.4 Overlap of Specific Learning Difficulties and Dyslexia

Amanda Kirby

Dyslexia often overlaps with other specific learning difficulties in up to 40% of individuals. These other specific learning difficulties may include Dyspraxia (also known as Developmental Co-ordination Disorder), Autism Spectrum Disorders (ASD), and Attention Deficit Hyperactivity Disorder (ADHD), and speech and language impairments. This may impact on how the person performs in tasks in the workplace or in managing to be self organised.

Not all individuals with Specific Learning Difficulties will be identified in childhood. For many individuals with Specific Learning Difficulties, their difficulties may have remained hidden and not been clearly identified. They may have been seen as not bothering with education, or may have become disenfranchised from society or even ended up in the penal system. Alternatively they may have struggled through alone or with additional support, but with far greater effort than their peers. Other individuals may have been identified during their childhood, have received help and need this to be continued in either the training or workplace setting. By identifying and addressing their specific needs this may mean the opportunity to reach their potential.

The umbrella term "Specific Learning Difficulties" (SpLD) is used to cover a wide variety of difficulties. Many people use it synonymously with Dyslexia (a difficulty with words), but it is now generally accepted that Dyslexia is only one of a group of difficulties that may include:

DCD (Developmental Co-ordination Disorder) also known as Dyspraxia - motor difficulties.

ADHD (Attention Deficit Hyperactivity Disorder) and ADD (Attention Deficit Disorder) - attention and concentration difficulties.

Dyslexia - reading and spelling difficulties.

Dysgraphia - writing difficulties.

Dyscalculia - a specific mathematics difficulty.

Speech, language and communication difficulties including Asperger's Syndrome and Autism Spectrum Disorder.

In addition, other mental health disorders such as Anxiety, Depression, Oppositional Defiant Disorder (ODD), Obsessional Compulsive Disorder (OCD) and Conductive Disorder (CD) may overlap with these conditions. Tourette's Syndrome may also overlap with these conditions.

What are the Key Symptoms and Signs?

ADHD: Attention Deficit Hyperactivity Disorder

ADHD affects about 1% of the population and can result in difficulties with skills such as organisation and time management. Some individuals feel fidgety or may need to move around. In adults this may not be obvious but could be seen in individuals "toe tapping" or "pen chewing" for example. Adults sometimes describe themselves as "internally" restless. Some individuals find it difficult to hold onto what they need to say in a conversation, for example, and may appear impulsive in answering out of turn. This may make it harder for them to be able to take their turn in a conversation. The individual may have poor attention to detail and may start various tasks but find it harder to complete them, as they may appear to become bored. Poor concentration may also be seen, drifting from one project to another for example. Time management and prioritisation may be harder to do. Individuals may appear to be easily distracted either by others or by their environment.

These symptoms and signs may leave the person feeling frustrated as they know they may have the ability to do a task, but find that because of poor concentration they find it hard to stay on task to do so successfully. Support requires making sure the environment is organised and there is help with time management. Choosing the right workplace environment can ensure the individual can be successful.

Individuals with ADHD may be good at jobs that have variety and may be good at the overview rather than the detail.

Practical Support for the Workplace

- Help with organisational skills is important. This relates to personal organisation as well as workplace organisation.

- Clear guidelines on outcomes for tasks with time frames.

- Discuss the job description so the individual has clear guidelines on what is expected.

- If the individual is in an office, setting up desk space so it is away from the main thoroughfare and avoiding hot desking.

- Setting up the computer and syncing the diary with a mobile phone will allow reminders and tasks to be logged and alarms set to remind the individual of tasks that need to be completed or meetings to be attended.

- Reducing external noise where possible - if not, using headphones when the individual has to concentrate on a task.

- Choice of job is essential to allow for variety to reduce risk of 'boredom'.

- Set time frames for tasks and use 'to - do' lists

Developmental Co-ordination Disorder (also known as Dyspraxia)

These are difficulties that impact on co-ordination. Individuals may have a range of difficulties. These may include poor handwriting, difficulty if needing to balance, actions that may require smooth movement and undertaking tasks that require accurate timing, especially at speed. However, individuals may vary considerably and if they are shown what to do, with practice, may acquire the skills to do most tasks. Learning to drive a car may be harder for the individual to do, and learning on an automatic car may be a better option.

The individual may have difficulties with office tasks such as filing, using a photocopier, for example, and may need to initially do these tasks more slowly until they have practised. Additionally for some, handling money or change in a shop may be slower to do. Recording information accurately because of poor handwriting may be harder to do. However with practice or alternative supports such as using a computer the individual may be able to do most tasks. Tasks that require speed and accuracy may be harder for the individual and may need a risk assessment. Some individuals with DCD may appear socially less confident because of less practice and so may need to be given some support to gain confidence working in a team.

Individuals with DCD may be empathetic and may have good skills working with children, elderly people and animals.

Practical Advice for the Workplace

- Applications for jobs should be able to be completed online and accepted in computer printed format. Avoid asking for handwritten letters.

- At interview offer additional time for responses, list key questions to be given before interview. Allow a colleague to attend if this is required.

- Risk assessment may need to be undertaken if fine motor tasks are required, especially at speed.

- Use computers to minimise the need for handwriting.

- When demonstrating new tasks or equipment, break down the tasks and allow additional practice and time to learn a new skill.

- Use techniques such as photos or pictures to show how skills are to be performed and as an aide memoir.

- Help setting up organisational systems such as use of Microsoft Outlook, using a mobile phone as a reminder for appointments.

- Avoidance of hot desking so the individual has their work possessions around them and in the same place.

Asperger's Syndrome /Autism Spectrum Disorders (ASD)

These are social and communication difficulties. They form a spectrum of disorders so that different individuals with the same diagnosis may have differences between them in their skills and deficits.

The main difficulties are an impairment in social interaction which impacts on socialising with others in all situations. The individual may have difficulty changing their social interaction depending on who they are with or where they are. This could result in appearing "distant" with someone they have met before or over- familiar with a stranger. It makes it harder for the individual to be adaptable and flexible, especially in new situations. Individuals may have a narrower range of hobbies and interests and may find it harder to make "social chit chat" and may appear rude at times if they come "straight to the point". They may interrupt others and talk too long on one topic. Use of idioms in conversation may be taken literally (such as "pull yourself together"). The individual may be more socially isolated from peers. They may appear to lack empathy and not pick up on non- verbal messages that allow the individual to recognise when others are angry, happy or upset. This may include not being aware of how far/near to stand when talking to others. There may be a greater risk of anxiety and depression.

Individuals with ASD may be excellent time keepers, follow through on tasks given, and be very loyal to their employer, always turning up to work and completing their work carefully.

Practical Advice for the Workplace

- It is important that the individual has information on the interview process prior to interview and the type of questions that may be asked in order to prepare.

- Allowing a colleague to attend with the individual for interview if necessary.

- Discuss the job description so that the individual has a clear understanding of what is expected. Discuss implicit social rules (i.e. the ones that are not obvious) e.g. when lunch is to be taken, dress code, how to address superiors.

- Make a list of acronyms that are used in the workplace with their meanings.

- Set up a time to review the job and if there are any misunderstandings, especially where there may be areas of ambiguity over job roles.

- Set routines where possible and inform where possible about changes that may occur.

- Avoiding hot desking if possible.

- Discussing (with permission) with work colleagues the social and communication difficulties so they do not misconstrue honesty with an appearance of being rude.

1.5 Case Study

Arran Smith, Proprietor of Azco Services

Dyslexia to me is now a gift; but it is also a hindrance. I found out I was dyslexic when I was about eight years old. Around the same time the dentist said to me let's take some teeth out. Being an eight year old I was quite excited, but would you like having your teeth taken out? This is how dyslexia felt for me over the next eight years.

Mom and Dad were very supportive, if it wasn't for them I wouldn't be where I am today. Mom took me to the Leicestershire Dyslexia Association where I had lessons in English and on computers. This built up my confidence because I could meet other dyslexic people and know that I wasn't alone. The years went on and I got more involved in the Association and I started working in the computer room. Then I started helping in our work shop and also helped in the teaching of Study Skills and organising events. The Committee then made me Vice-Chairman of the Association. The Chairman encouraged me to attend BDA meetings where I learned that there is a bigger world of dyslexia.

Dyslexia is a big part of my life. I still have my problem but I get around it by simply asking questions to people, how to spell this out, how do you spell that. The difficult part is having to get all my good ideas out of my brain on to paper, which is the most frustrating part of my dyslexia. But I am passionate about the cause; we need to know more about dyslexia in this world. I became a trustee of the BDA and am now at the forefront of dyslexia where I can support others, widen the awareness about dyslexia, and improve the understanding and attitude of society.

1.6 Forces for Change in the Workplace

Margaret Malpas, Chair, British Dyslexia Association

Arriving at the BDA and learning that the vision was "to create a dyslexia friendly world" seemed like a very big task. Early conversations began with talk about the crucial need for school teaching to be dyslexia friendly, but then another consideration arose, "What about the adults?" A quick investigation on what we did for adults, showed that the national landscape was very patchy.

We have a few very successful initiatives with adults through our Local Association network. Our Helpline receives nearly half of its enquiries and an increasing number of phone calls from adult dyslexics who are anxious about their job security. The Disability Student Allowance has created an awareness of the need to support students with dyslexia doing a first degree, yet this didn't seem to enable them to use the full range of coping strategies in their first job. There was some significant funding available through Access to Work but everyone trying to use this appeared to get offered the same solution and it took an inordinate amount of time between making an application and the solution.

However, this all indicated that the conversion to dyslexia friendly workplaces had scarcely begun. In any arena, to create change, even before objectives can be set and monitored, there has first to be an awareness that change is necessary and a willingness to engage and make that change happen. So creating awareness and the motivation to change were our first steps and these fitted very well with our training and conferencing.

The law, which sets the minimum standards, is specific on the requirements with respect to dyslexia in the workplace. The Disability Discrimination Act (2005) requires employers to make reasonable adjustments so that individuals with dyslexia can access work. Cases such as Patterson*and Brooking* proved that the law covered dyslexia at all levels and also that all the usual components at work, such as training and promotion, needed to be made accessible through reasonable adjustments.

It also places a duty to make services and products accessible to customers with dyslexia. This often comes as a surprise to employers where little has been done to address this so far.

The current case with Tesco* concerning pin number recognition in using debit and credit cards, which places a considerable strain on working memory for some, will no doubt further highlight legal responsibilities in this area.

To respond to these changes in a positive manner, the BDA initially developed a course for employers covering the law and how to make the workplace dyslexia friendly. The aim is to reach as many as possible and to this end, we have kept our prices low as a charitable activity. During the past year we have run a number of these awareness courses for employers within easy reach of most of England and Wales. This has worked extremely well in both creating an awareness of the condition and an appreciation that change in the workplace is necessary. Reactions have usually been total surprise at the extent of the condition within the population and that it covers such a wide spectrum of strengths and weaknesses. We always ask delegates on our courses to complete a course assessment sheet at the end of each workshop and I always scrutinise these for quality assurance purposes.

Imagine my delight when I saw the following on one just a year ago "I'm going back to make dyslexia awareness and support our number one objective for this year". This was written by the training manager in a large company related to the construction industry, where we knew there would be many hidden dyslexic individuals. Good to his word, he did just that and so now their courses are dyslexia friendly and awareness is spreading even more widely. Participants in our training have become some of our most active ambassadors championing the talents and needs of dyslexic employees.

In order to accelerate the pace of preparation for change, we have tried hard to ensure that our training dovetails with other BDA activities. One such is conferencing, and if you came to the Employers' Conference on the 9th March, you would have been able to hear exactly what happened when the training manager made dyslexia awareness his number one objective. This was the first BDA conference for employers, and arose naturally when we saw employers' reactions to the training. Once employers realised their responsibility for making adjustments for dyslexic employees, they wanted to hear how others were doing it.

From this we were able to ask those we knew were leading the field to come and tell others how they were making their organisations dyslexia friendly. The consequence of this was that we had a full line up of representatives from 12 large scale employers covering many industry sectors coming to tell their story, an exhibition of the latest in reasonable adjustments and the Minister for Work and Pensions agreeing to come and launch the whole event! Another significant step in the process towards change where employers could learn that change was needed.

We have also worked closely with our Helpline. They receive emails and telephone calls from many who face problems they do not know how to tackle. This has given us a good agenda of issues that we know require answers, which informs our content list for the courses. From this and feedback on the courses, we developed our subsequent courses, Making Reasonable Adjustments and Screening for Dyslexia. Participants often ask "what is reasonable?" and, as with most things in the dyslexia world, there is no definitive answer to this question. The condition can bestow a whole menu of possible strengths and weaknesses and consequently, every individual with dyslexia is different. It would, of course, be much easier if we could give employers a one stop solution in adjustments for their employees with dyslexia but this is simply not possible.

This fact is one that employers are now beginning to grapple with.

Assessing for reasonable adjustments for dyslexia is a specialist area and employers are advised to seek help from workplace dyslexia consultants or Access to Work.

So one year in, how are we doing on creating dyslexia friendly workplaces? Well, we have provided awareness training to over 5,000 people. The law has established minimum standards and with the new Equality Bill due in April this year which we have actively campaigned on, there will be a more consistent message on what is required. There will also probably be tougher requirements on disability discrimination, especially indirect discrimination.

Some of the loopholes such as the ability to avoid making adjustments on nebulous health and safety grounds will have been removed.

We will continue to work with Access to Work to reduce bottlenecks in the system of support to making adjustments. We have also worked with some employers who are leading the field in offering adjustments. These include Lloyds TSB who are providing assistive software as a matter of course for all employees (on the basis that what is good for dyslexic individuals tends to benefit all); also PricewaterhouseCoopers who are leading the way in establishing support networks in the workplace, to be followed by West Midlands Police and Ernst and Young. In summary, the process of awareness and motivation for change is under way. We are now working for real progress following fast on the heels of the early crusaders.

*Patterson v Commissioner of Police for the Metropolis.

*Brooking v Essex Police.

*Arnold case v Tesco.

1.7 A Snapshot of Dyslexia from a Research Perspective

Joel B. Talcott

Dyslexia engages the interest of a wide-range of stakeholders, from the children and adults who experience literacy difficulties, through the parents, educators and employers who work with them, to the scientific community that aims to understand the underlying causes of disability and the avenues for which intervention approaches might be most fruitful. This brief review aims to provide the reader with a flavour of current research perspectives on dyslexia. It is one of the most frequently diagnosed of the learning disabilities and will therefore be regularly encountered in occupational settings.

What is Dyslexia?

In the past, dyslexia was considered in some circles to be more a convenient social construction, created in part by parents to excuse their underperforming children, rather than a valid condition. This argument has recently been rekindled, despite an overwhelming body of scientific evidence to the contrary. It is now clear that dyslexia is a genetically influenced and neurobiologically based syndrome that is primarily manifest as a specific disorder of reading, characterised by literacy achievement that is substantially below that which would be expected for a person's chronological age and educational history (APA, 2000). Dyslexia persists into adulthood (see Everatt, this publication); in a recent study, over three quarters of children identified with specific reading difficulties in childhood had spelling in the lowest 3% of the population when re-assessed in adulthood (Rutter, Kim-Cohen & Maughan, 2006).

How is Dyslexia Diagnosed?

Diagnoses of dyslexia are usually made by professionals with accreditation in either clinical, educational or neuro-psychology and are based primarily on identifying reading difficulties on standardised tests of individual achievement in the absence of other obvious causes, such as substantially reduced cognitive skills or lack of access to education (see Beaton, 2004; Pennington, 2009; Snowling, 2000 for further reference). Because a range of environmental, behavioural and neurological factors are ruled out as potential causes of the reading difficulties, diagnosis is based heavily upon exclusionary criteria. This means that, aside from a measured difficulty in reading achievement, the symptoms associated with dyslexia can be very diverse. Thresholds for determining whether the reading difficulties are severe enough to warrant diagnosis often differ and can be defined by pragmatic and seemingly rather arbitrary statistical criteria. This has undoubtedly contributed to the wide range of prevalence estimates for dyslexia found in the literature. Depending upon the cut-off score adopted, between 3 and 8% of the population have reading difficulties of a dyslexic nature (Yule, Rutter, Berger & Thompson, 1974; Shaywitz, et al, 1992). This means that there are currently in excess of 3 million individuals with dyslexia in the UK, with approximately 24,000 new cases diagnosed per annum. Hence, dyslexia poses clear economic challenges for social and mental health later in life. In 2005, the Dyslexia Institute estimated that poor adult literacy alone cost the UK economy upwards from £1 billion per year.

Epidemiological Factors

More males than females (~1.5:1) are diagnosed with dyslexia (Rutter et al., 2004), with increasing numbers of boys identified when clinic-based rather than educational samples are used. This latter result is probably linked to a bias in referrals based on other aspects of behaviour that are common in boys (for e.g., inattention, hyperactivity) and often co-occur, but are not necessarily causally linked, with the reading difficulties that are also present. Up to 50% of persons with dyslexia diagnoses will also fulfil the criteria for a co-diagnosis of another developmental difficulty such as attention deficit disorder, developmental co-ordination disorder, specific language impairment or dyscalculia (Kadesjö & Gillberg, 2001; Kaplan, Wilson, Dewey & Crawford, 1998; Wilcutt et al., 2005). Thus, individual differences in the behavioural manifestations of dyslexia may result from the co-occurrence of different developmental disabilities. Yet, the constellation of symptoms associated with dyslexia alone can also extend well beyond those normally linked with language and literacy skills (see Beaton, 2004; Habib, 2000). The extent to which the co-diagnosis of these different types of disability is due to common underlying mechanisms or the overlap between separate disability types is currently a topic of intense research investigation (see for e.g., Ben-Ari, 2008).

Core Symptoms

The main cognitive mechanisms underlying the reading problems characteristic of dyslexia are linked to difficulties in learning the unique mappings between letter units and speech sounds and how knowledge of this code can be generalised to successfully read novel words (see Snowling, 2000; Everatt, this publication). The difficulty of this task is compounded in English especially, because these mappings from spelling to sound (and vice versa) are far less regular than those found in other languages, for example German & Spanish (Smythe et al., 2008). Correspondingly, speed and fluency of word reading are typically more problematic for dyslexic readers in languages with consistent mappings than is reading accurately (Serrano & Defior, 2008). Diagnosis of reading difficulties therefore focuses much more on these variables than word decoding skills in these more regular languages. The inconsistency of the letter sound mappings in English may also have potential knock on effects for spelling even in highly compensated adult readers with a history of dyslexia. Such readers may inconsistently apply spelling rules for novel words (Kemp, Parrilla & Kirby, in press). Alternatively, children with dyslexia may over-consistently apply spelling rules, even if they are inappropriate, in a similar way to beginning readers at a younger age (Bourassa & Treiman, 2008). The profile of reading difficulties not only varies across languages, but it also differs across individuals within a language. An example is that problems with phonological skills may be accompanied by additional difficulties in reading comprehension, but such difficulties can also occur in isolation from one another (Nation & Snowling, 1997). Recent research has confirmed that early phonological skills strongly predict reading accuracy but not reading fluency (Puolakanaho, et al., 2008). Collectively, these observations suggest that the presence of reading problems associated with word recognition can be quite separate from those related to deriving meaning from text. This highlights the need for organisations to both appreciate and evaluate the needs of poorer readers with respect to the literacy abilities demanded by their employment role.

Understanding the Genetic and Neurological Basis of Dyslexia

Dyslexia occurs within a developmental context. Individual profiles of strengths and difficulties within the domain of reading may therefore vary quite substantially. These individual differences are shaped substantially by both genetic and environmental factors (for example, in the adoption of compensatory reading strategies). It is in the appreciation of the biological basis of dyslexia that understanding of typical and atypical reading has been especially pronounced, owing in part to striking advances in neuroimaging and molecular genetic technology. An ever increasing body of literature is confirming that dyslexia is highly familial and heritable with genetic factors accounting for upwards of 50% of the variance in reading skills across the population (Fisher & DeFries, 2002). These findings alone should put to rest any debate that dyslexia is a myth.

From an evolutionary standpoint, reading is a relatively new behaviour in the human repertoire, hence there has been insufficient time for genes specific for reading to develop. Instead, multiple genes contribute to dyslexia susceptibility, with the strongest evidence pointing to several independent regions on separate chromosomes (Williams & O'Donovan, 2006). Importantly, the genes implicated in dyslexia are generally the same as those associated with reading skills within the normal range (Paracchini, et al., 2008). This supports the idea that reading differences between good and poor readers can be best understood in terms of quantitative differences rather than qualitative ones. Several of these genes have been shown to be involved in processes by which early development of the brain is regulated. Alterations in the functioning of these genes may result in delayed development of the neural architecture that supports reading. The brain is highly adaptable, however, and there is some evidence that appropriate training may in part normalise the brain network that is used for reading in children with dyslexia (Temple et al, 2003). Advances in non-invasive neuroimaging techniques now allow us to evaluate and track neural development in children. This will eventually yield data on the normative time-courses and developmental trajectories associated with reading development. Ultimately this will facilitate the development of more sensitive methods for early assessment, and thereby facilitate programmes of individually tailored intervention at the earliest time possible.

Conclusions

Dyslexia is far from a mythical construct. Although the manifestations of dyslexia at an individual level are highly variable, there is a well established genetic and neurological basis for reading difficulties. Careful consideration of the aetiology of poor reading firmly points in most cases to a core difficulty associated with the acquisition and use of phonological skills. Behavioural profiles within the domain of reading are highly influenced by an array of genetic and environmental factors. This highlights the need for organisations to appreciate the nature and needs associated with reading strengths and weaknesses at an individual level.

References

American Psychiatric Association. (2000). *Diagnostic and statistical manual of mental disorders* (4th ed., text rev.). Washington, CD: Author.

Beaton, A.A. (2004). *Dyslexia, reading and the brain: A sourcebook of psychological and biological research.* Hove, UK: Psychology Press.

Ben-Ari, Y. (2008). *Neuro-archaeology: pre-symptomatic architecture and signature of neurological disorders. Trends in Neurosciences, 31,* 626-636.

Bourassa, D.C. & Treiman R. (2008). Morphological constancy in spelling: a comparison of children with dyslexia and typically developing children. *Dyslexia, 14,* 155-169.

Fisher, S & DeFries, J. (2002). Developmental dyslexia: genetic dissection of a complex cognitive trait. *Nature Reviews Neuroscience*, 3, 767-780.

Habib, M. (2000). The neurological basis of developmental dyslexia: An overview and working hypothesis. Brain, 123, 2373-2399.

Kadesjö, B., and Gillberg, C. (2001). The comorbidity of ADHD in the general population of Swedish school-age children. *Journal of Child Psychology and Psychiatry*, 42, 487-492.

Kaplan, B.J., Wilson, B.N., Dewey, D. & Crawford, S.G. (1998). DCD may not be a discrete disorder. *Human Movement Science*, 17, 471-490.

Kemp, N., Parrilla, R. K. & Kirby, J. R. Phonological and orthographic spelling in high-functioning adult dyslexics. *Dyslexia* (in press) DOI: 10.1002/dys.364 .

Nation, K & Snowling, M. (1997). Assessing reading difficulties: the validity and utility of current measures of reading skill. *British Journal of Educational Psychology*, 67, 359-370.

Paracchini, S., Steer, C.D., Buckingham, L.L., Morris, A.P., Ring, S., Scerri, T., Stein, J., Pembrey, M.E., Ragoussis, J., Golding, J. & Monaco, A.P. (2008). Association of the KIAA0319 dyslexia susceptibility gene with reading skills in the general population. *American Journal of Psychiatry*, 165, 1576-84.

Puolakanaho A, Ahonen T, Aro M, Eklund K, Leppänen PH, Poikkeus AM, Tolvanen A, Torppa M, Lyytinen H. (2008). Developmental links of very early phonological and language skills to second grade reading outcomes: strong to accuracy but only minor to fluency. *Journal of Learning Disabilities*, 41, 353-370.

EFALEX HAS MORE PUBLISHED TRIALS THAN ANY OTHER BRAND...

well done Efamol ✓

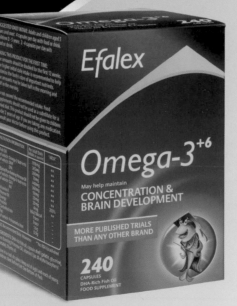

Efalex has more published trials than any other brand in relation to children's learning.

Taken every day, Efalex Omega-3 fish oil may help maintain concentration and brain development in children.

Need more information? Please visit **WWW.EFALEX.CO.UK**

Willcutt, E.G., Pennington, B.F., Olson, R.K., Chhabildas, N., & Hulslander, J. (2005). Neuropsychological analyses of comorbidity between reading disability and attention deficit hyperactivity disorder: In search of the common deficit. *Developmental Neuropsychology, 27, 35-78.*

Willliams, J. & O'Donovan, M. (2006). The genetics of developmental dyslexia. *European Journal of Human Genetics, 14, 681-689.*

Yule, W., Rutter, M., Berger, M & Thompson, J. (1974). Over-achievement and under-achievement in reading - distribution in general population. *British Journal of Educational Psychology, 44, 1-12.*

1.8 Research in Adults with Dyslexia

John Everatt

The area of dyslexia has often been considered in terms of its effects on children. However, dyslexic children grow up into dyslexic adults and, therefore, the effects of dyslexia on adults is also of concern to workers in the field. This brief overview provides a background to the sort of research that has considered the effects of dyslexia on adults. It covers a range of areas and, as such, can only provide a basic guide to the topic. However, the references cited should provide the reader with extra information.

Literacy Skills

The main feature of dyslexia in childhood is a problem with acquiring literacy skills, particularly word reading and spelling. Given this, it is hardly surprising to find that literacy problems extend into adulthood. However, the particular manifestation of literacy problems may vary between childhood and adulthood. For example, Miles (1993) suggested that reading accuracy may not be as good an indicator of dyslexia in adults as spelling ability. The adult dyslexic may be able to overcome some of the problems with reading accuracy that they showed in childhood. However, although reading accuracy may not be as bad as in childhood, reading speed still seems to be a problem for dyslexic adults. This means that reading may be accurate, but that the dyslexic adult seems to need much more time to decode words and may have to read text several times to access meaning (see Brooks et al, 2004).

In addition, for the child beginning to learn to read, word decoding may be the most important skill to learn. However, for the older individual, understanding text is the most important aspect of reading. Adults are rarely required to read out loud and accuracy may be a problem only when it interferes with comprehension. Therefore, strategies to support reading among adult dyslexics may be better focused on comprehension than decoding. The feature of adult dyslexics slowing down their rate of reading (or re-reading) seems to be related to the need to comprehend text. If reading is time-limited (i.e. the dyslexic cannot slow reading down), then comprehension suffers. If reading is not time-limited, then comprehension can be as good amongst dyslexic adults in education as it is for their non-dyslexic peers. Strategies that slow reading down to allow the dyslexic to employ metacognitive skills to understand text (e.g. asking questions about text, highlighting key words, etc.) seem to improve reading amongst adult education dyslexics more than strategies that focus on the word level skills. Therefore, the methods employed to support literacy may need to vary between childhood and adulthood.

Phonological Skills, Speed of Information Processing and Working Memory

The dominant causal hypothesis for the word level literacy problems discussed above is that dyslexics have problems processing sounds within words - they have a phonological processing deficit (see Snowling, 2000). This deficit in childhood is hypothesized to lead to problems decoding letter sequences. When presented with a new string of letters (such as SPLOOG), one way of reading this is to sound out the individual letters, combine the sounds into something that is word-like and pronounce this. Hence recognising sounds within words and decoding new letter strings are found to be weaker amongst dyslexics than non-dyslexics, and this weakness can extend into adulthood.

If the child comes across a known word that they haven't seen written before (e.g., SCHOOL), then decoding into a verbal form should also allow them to access its meaning. Therefore, such processing may require the ability to store sounds for a short time while letters are decoded, and to access known verbal labels from memory. Therefore, phonological processing has also been implicated in the memory (particularly working memory) deficits found among dyslexic individuals - and again this can be found in adults as well as children. Similarly, accessing from verbal memory needs to be accomplished fluently (accurately and quickly to avoid taxing the processing system during reading). Therefore, speed of processing has also been implicated as a feature of dyslexia, potentially due to its relationship to phonological processing. (See discussions in Beaton et al, 1999.)

Emotional Effects

There are also areas where the consequences of dyslexia may become more apparent with age and, therefore, may show greater effects among adolescents and adults. For example, previous research has found evidence for dyslexics demonstrating higher levels of emotionality, including high levels of frustration and anxiety, low self-esteem and lack of confidence (see Miles & Varma, 1995). This can increase the likelihood of poor outcome in education but can then extend to problems in employment. Low self-esteem and poor emotional control can be a major problem for an individual in work, particularly at times of stress. Therefore, it is not surprising to find that those dyslexics who express an ability to control these features seem to be the more successful in employment (Gerber et al, 1992). There also seems to be an increased likelihood of finding difficulties associated with dyslexia among juvenile and adult prison populations, which has been considered to be due to the alienation and poor prospects of those suffering from educational exclusion, either explicitly due to school behaviour problems or implicitly due to unsuccessful learning methods (see Rack, 2005). This does not mean that dyslexia leads inevitably to emotional and behavioural problems. Rather, the increased incidence argues for the need to avoid these problems to begin with (by better educational methods) or to implement procedures to overcome these problems if they manifest (for example, it may be necessary to support older dyslexics with techniques for overcoming emotional/behavioural problems in addition to providing adult literacy programmes).

Abilities as well as Disabilities

There may also be consequences that might be considered positive rather than negative. One possible consequence of dyslexia being seen in terms of a medical diagnosis is that we can focus on the negative symptoms. Obviously, from the point of view of trying to support the dyslexic, this is a reasonable stance. However, it can lead to us forgetting that problems associated with dyslexia are as much a matter of culture as biology. If literacy was not as important as it is considered in the modern world, then dyslexia might not be such a problem. Also, the requirements of modern education systems to be literate may hide the abilities of the dyslexic in areas other than literacy (in the arts, for example). There is ample evidence of dyslexic adults excelling in visual and creative areas (West, 1991). Although the evidence for innate talents in these fields is equivocal, the fact that dyslexic adults can perform as well as, if not better than, their non-dyslexic peers argues for us to avoid considering dyslexia as purely a problem. Even if creative talents are a consequence of having to find alternative solutions to learning (see Everatt et al, 1999), dyslexic adults will still show skills that, in the right circumstances, will prove to be invaluable to society as well as a bonus to employers.

Conclusions

The studies reported indicate that there is quite a large overlap between dyslexia in childhood and that in adulthood. However, there are specific manifestations of dyslexia amongst adults that need to be considered, such as the move from accuracy to fluency problems and the consequences for emotional/behavioural problems and visual/creative talents. Dyslexia in adults, therefore, needs to be considered from the perspective of education but also general life skills. As such, interventions may need to support literacy, but may be more effective if they also focus on study and life skills.

References

Beaton, A, McDougall, S, & Singleton, C (Eds), (1997). Special issue: *Dyslexia in literate adults*, Journal of Research in Reading, 20 (1).

Brooks, P, Everatt, J & Fidler, R (2004). *Adult Reading Test (ART)*. London: Roehampton University of Surrey.

Everatt, J, Steffert, B, & Smythe, I (1999). An eye for the unusual: Creative thinking in dyslexia. *Dyslexia*, 5, 28-46.

Gerber, PJ, Ginsberg, R, & Reiff, HB (1992). Identifying alterable patterns in employment success for highly successful adults with learning disabilities. *Journal of Learning Disabilities*, 25, 475-487.

Miles, TR (1993). *Dyslexia: The Pattern of Difficulties* (second edition). London: Whurr.

Miles, TR, & Varma, V (1995). *Dyslexia and Stress*. London: Whurr.

Rack, J (2005). The incidence of hidden disabilities in the prison population: Yorkshire and Humberside research. *Dyslexia Review*, 16, 10-22.

Snowling, M.J. (2000). *Dyslexia*, second edition. Oxford: Blackwell.

West, TG (1991). *In the Mind's Eye*. *Buffalo*, New York: Prometheus.

John Everatt is a Professor in the School of Literacies and Arts in Education, University of Canterbury, New Zealand. email: john.everatt@canterbury.ac.nz

1.9 Dyslexia in the Workplace in Wales
Welsh Dyslexia Project

It is 8 years since Prosiect Dyslecsia Cymru / Welsh Dyslexia Project was 'born', with the aim to provide advice and support to dyslexic individuals, parents, carers, professionals working in the field of dyslexia, and also to employers and employees involved in the working environment. The ultimate goal is to make Wales a world leader as far as dyslexia is concerned!

We feel as an organisation that we are well along this path, having been actively involved in:

- Developing Welsh language and bilingual resources (both paper and IT based) for use at home and in schools across the Principality.

- Making available an e-learning course 'Teaching and supporting children and young persons with dyslexia', making use of a Virtual Learning Environment set up.

- Providing free of charge, a Welsh and an English Screening Test that can be used in school, and downloaded from our web site, (http://www.welshdyslexia.info) which shows whether a child in primary school is at risk of being dyslexic.

- Creating a bilingual CD that offers advice and strategies that can be used by parents at home, to support their dyslexic child.

- Developed with the support of Bangor University, a Welsh language text to speech word processing program called 'EdGair'.

- Working collaboratively with Claro Software in the development of a Welsh version of their mind-mapping Software: MindFull.

- Organising numerous workshops and conferences on dyslexia topics for the purpose of raising greater awareness and in keeping people in Wales up to date on ongoing developments and research.

- Setting up a bilingual Free-phone telephone helpline that operates Monday to Friday, with trained advisers who can offer advice as well as a 'listening ear' to those concerned about specific aspects of dyslexia or the graduated procedure for assessment etc. which is outlined in the SEN Code of Practice (Wales).

However, since March 2008, we secured a 2 year funding from the Big Lottery Fund (People and Places programme) enabling us to have a physical presence through an Advice and Resources Centre in Cardigan and the appointment of 2 part-time staff.

We have seen a vast increase in referrals to us in respect of dyslexia in Adults and in the workplace, and requests for either screening or assessment and also as to what assistive technology is available to support the dyslexic employee or those considered at risk, to help them overcome some of the problems they face. In Wales, we do not have an organisation such as ADO (Adult Dyslexia Organisation) as exists in England, whose aim is to "promote the cause of dyslexia through lobbying, research, training and campaigning."

We, therefore, feel as Prosiect Dyslecsia Cymru / Welsh Dyslexia Project, that we need to look at addressing the need in Wales, (as well as taking into account the Welsh language aspect within the working environment) and subject to our securing appropriate funding, to set up a support structure for both employers, employees, the unemployed or partially-employed.

We were amazed on enquiring of the Basic Skills-Wales that they have no input to addressing the needs of the dyslexic adult in Wales, and only concentrate on those individuals with low literacy and numeracy skills. We wonder whether there is a very fine dividing line here, and ask whether the low literacy and numeracy are brought about through the individual being dyslexic or dyscalculic?

Many of these adults may have missed being recognised whilst at school or college, and have been let down by the education system, and now the situation has significant implications for their working environment, where they face difficulties. PDC now regularly receives requests from employers and Human Resource Managers in Wales as to how they can adapt the place of work to help both the business itself and the employee.

Indeed, very few employers are aware of the fact that dyslexia is classed as a disability under the Disability Discrimination Act and that they are expected to make 'reasonable adjustments' so that dyslexic people are not significantly disadvantaged at work.

It is with this in mind, that we are going to place greater emphasis on Adult dyslexia and initially, organise a Conference and Workshop on Dyslexia in the Workplace, to which we aim to have a Welsh Assembly Minister with responsibility for employment and skills to give an address, as well as inviting organisations such as Department of Work and Pensions, Fire Service, Royal College of Nursing, Health Authority, Trade Unions, along with a Human Resources Manager from a Wales based company to give presentations.

We have already held discussions with assistive software specialists: Iansyst, Claro Software and Penfriend inviting them to have a presence at the Conference and to display and demonstrate the Assistive Technology hardware and software they have available to meet the specific needs of dyslexic people.

Having recently formed a partnership with Trinity College, Carmarthen (which is now Wales' latest University), we are looking at the possibility of research being undertaken on 'Dyslexia in the Workplace in Wales', which will give us specific information as to the incidence of dyslexia among employees.

With the right information, employers can help to create an inclusive environment ensuring that all differences are welcomed and that relevant support given to the dyslexic individual in her / his place of work.

PDC aims to highlight the fact that it is possible for individuals in the workplace not only to have a diagnostic assessment, but also a workplace needs assessment in order that they receive appropriate support, and the role that the Access to Work programme plays within Wales.

Michael Davies

(Trustee and Chief Executive in a voluntary capacity) of Prosiect Dyslexia Cymru /Welsh Dyslexia Project.
Email: llechryd1@btgconnect.com

1.10 Case Study

Edward Charvet, Co-founder of WLI, owners of
Trovus Revelations

For me, being classified as a dyslexic, has meant a lifetime
of oscillation between two emotional extremes. One end is a
self supporting reassurance based on the belief that I am not
doing too badly, considering. The other is the embarrassment
of not been able to consume the written word and disseminate
information as efficiently as "normal" people. This second
area is driven home all the more acutely now I am a father
of two young children. My 4 year old is now correcting my
reading mistakes and encourages me to speed up when
reading to him, as my disjointed ramblings do nothing to
enhance the storyline. What I am well aware of, though, is
the adaptive nature of the human form. What the mis-wiring
of my mental biology has taken away, nature gives back in
other areas. It is a well known fact that many dyslexics have
pronounced skills in other areas. Akin, I imagine, to the blind
person whose hearing becomes increasingly sensitive, I have
found that other forms of communication are improved so
that I can get my messages across. I don't lack for vocabulary
or the ability to formulate ideas and therefore in recent years
public speaking is something that I have become increasingly
accomplished at. This, combined with what I know as a high
Emotional Intelligence (EQ), mostly showing itself as an ability
to accurately read people and situations, gives me a wonderful
gift set that is carrying me through life. Education remains vitally
important and at the core of people's development. It is hard
not to be saddened by the ignorance of the comments currently
coming from elements of the Government relating to a dyslexic

epidemic. I managed to get to degree level, but not without the support and understanding of each institution along the way. I have found in later life that recognising my limitations as much as my strengths has allowed me to find a business partner who complements me and allows us together to grow our business by focusing on our strengths.

1.11 A European Policy Perspective

European Dyslexia Association

The European Dyslexia Association represents 42 national and regional organisations across Europe and is actively aware that there may be up to 25 million dyslexic adults within the EU who may be unemployed or under-employed.

This discussion paper will outline the ideological, cultural and policy differences around dyslexia which combine to limit progress on the topic. A range of issues need to be addressed in order to create coherent policy and practice across Europe.

Strategic analysis of ideological differences

At present, EU wide policy and legislation is based on the prevention of disability discrimination and in this context how discrimination affects disabled people in the workplace.

However, there is no consensus view that dyslexia is a disability. Many dyslexic adults refuse to accept the label of disabled as they come to terms with their own learning differences in a largely dyslexia-unfriendly world.

Some European countries are ambivalent on the same issue, and at a recent meeting of presidents of the EDA member organisations, it soon became clear that we do not share the view that dyslexia is a disability.

Moreover, the social model of disability which is now a long established concept is not universally known and therefore is not being applied to drive policy change. In short, the social model of disability prefers to see the individual with differences as "disabled" by the environmental, attitudinal and systemised barriers to their condition, impairment or difference.

The medical/traditional model of disability on the other hand views the person's differences, condition or impairment as a medical problem that needs to be "cured" or fixed in some way. From this standpoint, the person viewing the adult with differences reinforces and creates barriers to that person's assimilation into society and right to belong as an equal.

This is very evident in the world of work where disabled people experience unemployment at a rate of four times higher than non-disabled people. Much of this variation is explained by prejudicial attitudes that assume the disabled person cannot achieve all of the requirements of the post on offer.

Although the application of the social model of disability has arguably bought about significant and positive change for disabled people in the UK and Scandinavian countries, things are still far from ideal and there is much to be done. However, employment rates are improving and indeed the full range of occupational and educational opportunities are becoming more freely available as societal attitudes and acceptance of disabled people as fully contributing citizens influence policy.

For dyslexia however, this ideological position and policy direction is unclear. As mentioned there is no universal acceptance that dyslexia is a disability and unfortunately many "treatments" have a medical bias that seek to "cure" dyslexia. Without taking up valuable space by citing examples, the EDA is confident that all readers will have come across practitioners or companies offering "miracle cures".

Policy Concerns

The context for research in the dyslexia field has highlighted significant differences of opinion relating to causation, definition and, as a consequence, the best ways to support blue and white collar workers with dyslexia.

Again I am not going to provide an overview of the differences in understanding but make the point that vibrant debate in the public eye may be good for researchers who wish to sell books and companies wishing to promote their "therapy", but the picture created does little to influence policy makers in the EU who see the dyslexia world as discordant and lacking consensus on key points of debate.

Failure to agree core elements fosters a disparate voice and increasingly a disenfranchised movement despite the very high numbers of people with dyslexia in Europe. For the individual concerned there is real risk of an unfulfilled and unproductive lifestyle.

Former IBM European President and President of the German Industries Hans-Olaf Henkel's statement to the question at the 16th Federal Conference of the German EDA member Bundesverband Legasthenie October 2008: "Can the economy afford to renounce 10 percent of reliable school graduates?" - "No, indeed!" ("but ...")

At a national level, there are further variations of approach that negatively impact on European wide policy change.

Despite the very significant numbers of adults with dyslexia in Europe, there are some countries that do not recognise dyslexia. This is in part practical, in terms of language acquisition in those countries but may also represent cultural beliefs. Many countries in Europe are child centred regarding dyslexia which is to be applauded, if this leads to early identification and intervention.

However, the development of policy and services for children has often been at the expense of service development and awareness raising for the adult dyslexic population who, in any case, probably represent two-thirds of the dyslexia need within the country. Sometimes the concentration on children's services negatively reinforces an institutionally based provision, which in turn plants policy seeds for the dyslexic adult of tomorrow.

There are also language differences, not in the obvious sense but more in the appropriateness of terms and words we use concerning dyslexia. For example, in the UK referring to a disability as a "handicap" is increasingly rare. The term handicap derives from charitable aid at a time when the disabled person may go "cap in hand" to seek financial support. Therefore referring to a "handicapped" person is insulting and suggests that the individual may not be financially independent and require charity. The subtleties and nuances of this word and other related language is not shared across Europe where in 2009 some countries refer to handicapped citizens without inhibition.

The Task of the European Dyslexia Association

It is therefore imperative that the EDA can provide a common vision from the variances of knowledge, understanding and acceptance of dyslexia across Europe. Our vision represents people who experience dyslexia as equal citizens with skills and competencies that can make a very positive contribution to the world at large. It is only when people are valued as unique with equal rights that we will begin to see fairer representation and access to education, employment and enterprise.

We face a number of choices and decisions in order to strengthen the voice of dyslexia in Europe. The role of the EDA is to facilitate country by country development and where needed, exert influence in the European Parliament and the European Commission. It is probably in the field of dyslexia and employment that we face our biggest challenges.

There is no doubt that the number of people who experience dyslexia form a massive lobby for change and a current potential for waste, as talent and ability go unsupported. This is both a moral outrage as well as an economic one in that even in the current global recession, no country can afford to ignore this group and must utilise its capability.

The dyslexia world cannot stay as a fragmented voice, uncertain in its reach and parameter and unclear on what change is necessary. During the 21st century there is a commitment to develop policy and practice based on promoting equality and inclusion and underpinned by the acceptance of diversity.

This must lead to a major paradigm change in thinking, away from the negativity of models that segregate and separate and from a language that devalues and insults.

The EDA therefore has a vital role, to seek to provide a common platform to secure long lasting policy change to unite European countries and ensure that all dyslexic people achieve their ambition in employment, training and in all aspects of life.

1.12 Giving Hope in the USA
Glenn Young

In 2008, Buffalo, New York is a city deep in depression. Many of those who remain in the city are unemployed or underemployed, and many women with children remain on the US "welfare" programs (or Aid to Families with Dependent Children) as almost their only source of income. Public and private social services agencies (or "charities" in the UK) struggle to provide some basic support services to keep families barely afloat in these on-going difficult times. The largest of these agencies nationally is Goodwill Industries.

It would not be considered likely that in such an environment, of "triage" services provided by Goodwill in Buffalo, that we would expect to find signs of hope for new approaches to the needs of women with dyslexia (or as stated in the US, learning disabilities). And yet, through a program called LIVES (Linking Individuals with VESID Employment Services - VESID being the New York State Vocational Rehabilitation Program) this is exactly what we are finding; a new approach to addressing the needs of women on welfare with dyslexia/LD. In this program, very poor women are being:

■ Recognised, often for the first time, as having dyslexia/LD,

■ Connected to appropriate services for persons with disabilities(through the US Vocational Rehabilitation System), and

■ (Often for the first time in their lives) Make progress in their personal vocational success as they are get services aimed at employment success, and not just "literacy improvement."

Over the course of the last six years, the LIVES program has become a working model of success. These new "openings" and "opportunities" for these women with dyslexia/LD through LIVES came about as a result of years of effort and research that has laid bare the false notions that have for decades dominated the fields of dyslexia/LD, as well as the fields of welfare and workforce development.

■ The new research has shown clearly that these fields, at least in the US, greatly under-identified the numbers of persons with dyslexia/LD, and that those who were mainly not identified have been females, especially poor females, and especially poor women of ethnic origin.

This lack of identification has had profound impact on the lives of individuals not identified; but also has often rendered large scale public efforts at worker retraining and employment development failures. These programs often assumed that the issues of "failure" for these women were based in "motivation" and not the real issue of unidentified dyslexia/LD.

The root of this failure to identify lay in the structure and design of the special education system in the US. However, the history of dyslexia/LD in the special education setting in the US is beyond the scope of this paper. Without describing the problems involved, we can now clearly state, based on national data and new research, that:

■ Since about 1980 some 5% of children in US schools have been classified as children with "LD", this rate has under-identified the actual number of children with dyslexia/LD by perhaps 200% (the actual rate may be 15% as opposed to 5%); and

- That the vast majority of those not identified are low income children, especially low-income females.

In addition, this limited view of children with dyslexia/LD (the "five percent view") extended into a distorted view of the make up of the adult dyslexic populations (we see it as predominantly male and white. For example see Hoffman et al 1987.)

We can now trace the impact of the lack of identification in schools of poor women, and particularly poor women of ethnic origin, dyslexia/LD to ongoing long term economic failures. In addition, research shows a strong relationship between this disability and teen pregnancy and early motherhood. And, in the US, to what is called "welfare dependency".

Sparked by research papers on the gender bias in identification of dyslexia/LD and its potential link to welfare, during the 1990's several US states undertook projects to address the issue of unidentified dyslexia/LD within in their "welfare programs". Through these state projects and other research, by the early 2000's the US Federal government recognized that as many as half of those women on state support for "dependent children" (the US welfare programs) had unidentified dyslexia/LD.

These reports stated that not addressing the dyslexia/LD continued the pattern of fails for these women. But these reports also cited a new major problem based in the "welfare reform" of the late 1990's; the reports stated, that perhaps hundreds of thousands of women every year were beginning "sanctioned off" welfare due to their inability to make progress in employment and training, based in the manifestations associated with dyslexia/LD.

Across the board, these state projects yielded similar overriding findings; these "welfare moms"

- Were not "self aware" that they had dyslexia/LD; and

- Were clearly being impacted by the manifestations of the disability, in welfare settings and work settings, and

- Were clearly being impacted by "gender specific" issues related to dyslexia/LD (such as in the area of pregnancy and birth control).

Prompted by these reports, as well as Federal government "guidance" statements and successful law suits on behalf of the women being sanctioned (based in US disability law), the LIVES program was developed in New York State to both better meet the needs of these women and to try and stop this "sanctioning" from occurring.

The scope of the LIVES program is limited by time and resources issues, however; now, through LIVES, all persons coming onto welfare in Buffalo are "screened" for dyslexia/LD. The screening is administered by staff specifically trained in dyslexia/LD issues.

The data on the six years of screening process shows some 75% of those screened to have strong indicators of dyslexia/LD. The "at risk" populations fall into three main subgroups; those who were:

- Never identified with dyslexia/LD in schools (about 60%).

- Identified in school and received essentially poor services, but still connect the concept of dyslexia/LD to bad school and work experiences (about 15%).

- Identified at some point but received little or no services anywhere and did not connect the concepts of dyslexia to issues of work or school failures (25%).

After screening, there is counselling for the "moms" about dyslexia/LD, and persons are presented with the option of obtaining formal diagnostic testing (without charge) by the VESID.

The staff also introduce the women to the concepts of "reasonable accommodations" (US term equivalent to the UK term of "reasonable adjustments"). Part of the counselling involves helping the person to accept that these "accommodations" are legitimate and accommodations are not a form of "cheating".

■ In the relatively safety of Goodwill, perhaps for the first time, these women are allowed to start to use the "assistive technology" and other accommodated approaches in a workplace setting that can lead to on going employment success.

Therefore, through LIVES, these women are becoming "self aware" that they do have dyslexia/LD and that there are readily available "socially acceptable" means to become more successful, by accepting the fact that they have dyslexia/LD. This has proven to be a major step forward for these women and has been shown to be a foundation from which to build upon. With the new base, many of these women evolved out of the "Goodwill level job." Many entered community colleges, and job training programs with the support of "disability services" in these colleges. In addition, based on the women's ability to declare "disability status," many are now open about the disability in their new work settings, and have the employer's recognition and acceptance of the disability.

■ The LIVES program data shows that over the life of the project participants' long-term employment rates are over 70% (as compared to low 30's for other types of welfare work programs.).

The LIVES success that we find in this poor Buffalo setting seems to lie in the fact that the model and service approach is one that is:

■ Based directly on the needs and the background of these "welfare moms"; and

■ Does not try to impose other "dyslexia/LD models for success" based on the older paradigm of dyslexia/LD (the white male models); and

■ Does not try to "fix" the person's illiteracy, but instead to work with the person to gain success by a far greater focus on "accommodations".

And perhaps most importantly, the LIVES programs helps its participants to understand what has so long been denied to them; the understanding that they have a disability. And with this understanding, the focus of gaining success for this population of low-income women with dyslexia/LD comes from use of the civil rights protections offered under the Americans with Disabilities Act, rather than a "hope" through "literacy instruction."

While developing this article I interviewed several women who are in the LIVES program and found remarkable similarities in their stories (abuse, lack of attending school, early aged motherhood). I also found strong indicators that this new approach was beginning to make positive changes in their own views of themselves.

Glenn Young is currently operating as a consultant on adult learning disabilities issues for several state and local government agencies working to improve the lives of all persons with learning disabilities involved in workforce and welfare programs. Please see his web site at www.glennyoungcsld.com

2. Assessing Strengths and Weaknesses

2.1 The Assessment of Dyslexic Adults

David McLoughlin, Independent Dyslexia Consultants, British Dyslexia Association Organisational Member.

Introduction

One of the keys to success in employment for dyslexic adults is understanding. This has two dimensions:

- The extent to which dyslexic people are understood by their employers.

- The extent to which a dyslexic individual understands themselves.

The assessment process is fundamental to both and should allow for the determination of solutions that lead to effective performance. A comprehensive assessment can contribute to the most positive outcome for both employer and employee.

Types of Assessment

There are essentially two types of assessment:

(i) Screening - this can consist of checklists such as those published on websites, individually administered scales such as the Dyslexia Adult Assessment Test (DAST) and computer based tests such as the Lucid Adult Dyslexia Screening test

(LADS). Essentially screening confirms in a systematic way that some of the characteristics associated with dyslexia are evident. It can be conducted by people with varied professional backgrounds.

(ii) A diagnostic Assessment - establishes what people can do in terms of their ability, shows what they have achieved in terms of the development of their literacy and numeracy skills, as well as explain inconsistencies between expectation and performance. This is usually conducted by a psychologist. Some specialist teachers undertake diagnostic assessments but the tests available to them are less comprehensive than those used by psychologists.

Criteria for Dyslexia

The criteria for diagnosing dyslexia have been described as:

(i) Unexpected underperformance in a basic skill area such as reading, spelling and/or arithmetic.

(ii) Positive evidence of a difficulty processing information, e.g., in short term or working memory.

These must, however, be considered in the context of an individual's family, educational and occupational background. It is also important to be aware that sometimes discrepancies do not become evident until times of transition when demands have increased. Dyslexic people become a victim of their own success in that they reach levels in their work at which they do not have the skills they need to perform effectively, even though this has always been the case in the past. People do not suddenly become dyslexic and a good education can mask it because the obvious signs such as reading and spelling difficulties are not evident. It is now much better understood as a processing problem; 'literate dyslexic' is not an oxymoron!

Differential Diagnosis

The proper identification of dyslexia is through a process known as differential diagnosis. This attempts to isolate factors that explain why certain tasks are difficult for dyslexic people. It is similar to the process of elimination physicians use when trying to explain illness.

Following an interview in which details are taken of someone's medical, educational and occupational history are taken, the assessment usually begins with a comprehensive measure of intellectual or cognitive ability. Internationally, the widely used test is the Wechsler Adult Intelligent Scale. Although it is a measure of general intelligence, it is much more than this as it covers a range of abilities such as the understanding and use of language, verbal reasoning, non verbal reasoning, and spatial skills. It does therefore establish what individuals should be able to do. People with good verbal skills, for example, should ordinarily be expected to have well developed reading, writing and spelling skills as there is a relationship between the two. Verbal ability is also the arguably best guide to academic and employment success. Good non verbal skills relate to practical activities, including mathematics.

The Wechsler Scale also includes measures of working memory and processing speed. Typically, dyslexic individuals score less well on these than they do on the verbal and non verbal tests, and there are characteristic profiles of strengths and weaknesses.

Having established that there is an inconsistency amongst an individual's intellectual or cognitive abilities, some aspects of this are usually explored further. Visual memory, for example, is explored separately and tests that measure abilities often associated with literacy skills such as rapid naming are included.

Literacy Skills

Reading

Reading is usually assessed in a number of ways. Single word reading tests of continuous prose reading are used to measure accuracy. Arguably the most important reading skill during the adult years is silent reading comprehension and this is measured separately, as is silent reading speed. Other skills related to reading, such as proofreading are also measured.

Writing and Spelling

Spelling is usually measured by the administration of single word spelling tests. There are many of these appropriate to the adult years. It is however as important to examine spelling in the context of the writing of prose, as there is often deterioration in spelling when someone is having to think of more than just individual words. Writing is also examined for legibility, fluency, grammar and punctuation.

Numeracy

In some cases, numeracy is an important area for individuals in the workplace and separate tests of this can be administered.

Interpreting Test Scores

Test scores are expressed in a number of ways. The most common with adults is what are known as centile rankings. These establish how an individual compares with people of a similar age. It is however important to consider that as adults we only need the skills that we need. Sometimes therefore, relatively low centile rankings do not always mean that someone is unable to function in a particular job. Literacy skills can be rated as being at functional, vocational, technical and professional level. The last is what is required for university and beyond whilst the first is sufficient to allow one to read a tabloid newspaper. Vocational skills are those needed for semi-skilled work and the technical level is that associated with skilled manual work. The least appropriate way to rate skills in the adult years is using age scores; beyond adolescence it is only the extent of someone's reading vocabulary that becomes important.

Diagnosis

The diagnosis of dyslexia is based on the test scores as described above but within the context of medical, occupational and educational history. Dyslexia is usually genetic in origin and a family history of written language difficulties can be an important predictor.

Re-assessment

As much practice in the area of dyslexia has been developed through work with children it is not uncommon for policy and procedures to be based on this, often inappropriately. One example is re-assessment, adults sometimes needing to have a series of complete assessments to meet administrative criteria. There is a need for re-assessment but, if we acknowledge that dyslexia is genetic in origin, permanent but shows itself differently across the lifespan, all that is required once a diagnosis has been made is measurement of its effects such as current impact on reading so that relevant adjustments can be made. Dyslexic people do not need to be re-tested every two years!

Implications for Adjustments

If the adjustments employers make in the workplace are to level the playing field as well as establish equity, they should be based on the evidence provided by the assessment. Too often, solutions are just based on the fact that someone has been described as dyslexic. Technological solutions, for example, are often seen as a panacea. To be able to use a computer, however, it is necessary to be able to read and spell unless one has alternative assistive software such as voice recognition and text to speak packages.

Self Advocacy

The assessment process is also essential to an individual developing an understanding of their strengths and weaknesses, as well as the impact dyslexia is having on them. Even the most dyslexia friendly employer will not be an expert on how it affects a particular individual. The assessor can make recommendations but it is important that the dyslexic person themselves be able to advocate for themselves, explaining the difficulties they experience and offering solutions.

Further Reading

McLoughlin, D, Leather, C.A. and Stringer, P.E. (2002). *The adult Dyslexic: Interventions and Outcomes*. London:Whurr.

2.2 Identifying Skills for Careers and the Workplace

Sue Flohr, Helpline and Policy Manager, British Dyslexia Association

Why it is Important

Nobody has to be a round peg in a square hole. We can spend up to a third of our time in the workplace so we owe it to ourselves to get it right. Yet so many dyslexic people don't or don't think they know how to. There is an abundance of professional support about to guide and help us to decide upon a career but first of all, to get the best out of life, it helps to know what we enjoy and what we are good at. What is needed is forethought and planning. Our brains have around 200 billion neurons - more or less - but it is the way that they are wired up that gives us that unique opportunity to be different. We don't all look alike on the outside so we are not going be the same inside and this is where our plan becomes helpful.

Wondering about a Dream Job

The first step is to have an idea of what we want to do. We can write a list of questions to ask ourselves to clarify our ideas. The power of the imagination should not be overlooked either. Dreaming of our perfect future motivates us to bring about the change we want. So set aside the 'here and now' and start to create a view of the future world of work.

In 5 years time what would we like to be doing? Would our job be working closely with people, interacting with the public or customers? Would we want to be working in a team alongside others for support, or do we prefer to work alone? Do we like routine? Do we see ourselves in that perfect job in 5 years time having structure to our day or are we stifled by regularity and seek variety? Does staying in an office provide the security or would we prefer to be out and about? Do we enjoy interacting with the elderly or young people? Would we prefer to be providing back up office or IT support?

A useful metaphor can be to think of career development as a journey through the world of work acquiring new knowledge, skills and experiences along the way. We usually start a journey with a destination in mind, but how we get there may not always be clear. There are options of buses, trains, cycling or walking. Along the way we might see somewhere more appealing and divert. It is our personal journey to enjoy and experience what is on offer and available for each of us personally.

Understanding our Type of Learning Style

Then we need to think how to go about it. Even if we are sure that we know the path we want to follow, if we are dyslexic it is important to be aware of how we operate when practising proactive optimism.

Calls to our Helpline show that this is not always the case

Getting that all-important offer of an apprenticeship for plumbing seemed great for John until he realised that he had not escaped the reading and writing that he so hated at school. But with his ambition in sight he was ready to find out how to learn to learn.

An offer to study medicine was a dream come true for Mary. That was until the start of the course when she realised too late that she had been accepted onto a formally taught learning path rather than the self directed study one that she would have preferred.

Completing the BDA learning styles questionnaire can help us all if we are not quite sure how we learn:

Looking at these lists of activities related to each area of learning, think of our learning experiences. Try to identify activities which would suit us best. This can provide a rough guide to our learning style.

Auditory:

Digital recording.

Dictation.

Lectures.

Video conferencing.

Radio.

Discussion.

Using mnemonics to remember facts.

Taking part in debates.

Reading aloud.

Visual:

Computer based learning.

DVD's/TV.

Photographs.

Power Point presentations.

Pictures.

Diagrams.

Using interactive CD-Roms.

Using mind maps, flow charts.

Colour coding your notes.

Kinaesthetic:

Interactive CD-Roms.

Field Trips.

Computer based learning.

Activity based learning.

Visits.

Rehearsing and performing.

Using movement to stimulate memory.

Drawing diagrams and mind maps.

Using games.

We might need reassurance about the way that we operate and finding our learning style can help. We may need to brush up skills to take us successfully along our pathway and then it helps to investigate the way that we acquire our skills.

Choosing a Course for Professional Development:

Thinking about our learning will help us to research for an appropriate course:

■ How much reading will there be

■ Is it a coursework based programme

■ Will there be written examinations

■ Will spelling be assessed

■ Will it be self directed learning

- Will lectures be interactive or will we need to be able to concentrate for long periods listening

- Will we be able to write fast enough to take notes in lectures

- How will we get our ideas onto paper

Having gained our qualifications we are now prepared for the workplace.

Overcoming Barriers

Dyslexics have particular talents and skills which often go with predominantly being right brained with notable strengths resulting from their imaginative problem solving abilities. They are often creative, artistic and practical but this is not always the case. There is room for a diverse workforce in all areas especially when the barriers can be lifted. Albert Einstein famously said 'In the middle of difficulty lies opportunity'. The Government's Access to Work Scheme should help resolve difficulties and provide opportunities by making technical and human support available.

Every day our helpline is inundated with callers who find the difficulties have changed because the emphasis of their job has changed and they stumble, thinking that there is no way forward and that they must give up even when they have the skills for the job. We try to think of innovative ways to help them to continue or to make that all important change like the examples given here:

- John was devastated when he broke up with his partner. He enjoyed his job as a delivery driver but she had provided support as a co-driver, reading the road signs to help to overcome his multi-tasking difficulties. When he found out that he could be provided with a Sat Nav to replace her he was over the moon.

- Ann found that she was working way into the night after all her colleagues had left work simply because she couldn't concentrate during the day to get through her work. A sound blaster headset was provided to block out auditory distractions for her and now she can leave on time.

- Kuldeep was fed up being a taxi driver who got all the routine jobs but when his employer realised that the names of places and directions could be fed through to his iPhone and read aloud (rather than him having to depend upon reading back his poor handwriting and spelling and getting lost), his world changed.

- Mary wondered whether she should return to work as a zoo keeper for the council but, as age was creeping up on her, she preferred the indoor environment that her transfer to administration provided. Her worries over mastering her spelling issues were soon quashed when she found out that she could use voice activate software to overcome her spelling problem.

So it doesn't have to be a game of snakes and ladders. Getting it right in the first place with reasonable adjustments can help the dream come true.

2.3 Case Study

Chris Fortey, Multimedia Computer Programmer

I was lucky to have been sent to a good primary and secondary school, spending time at primary school on lessons with a special needs teacher. My secondary school also offered good support for special needs, offering things like reading clubs and at one stage tutors to sit in on classes. The special needs department was also able to explain my difficulties to other staff who thought that I was not working as hard as I could. I was supported in exams with extra time and a teacher was allowed to copy my answers and correct spellings and grammar.

College and university again supported me with extra time in exams as well as providing me with a personal tutor. I did well at college and passed my degree with a first classification.

Now, having had several jobs, I have found that people's understanding about dyslexia varies. While working for a sole trader, my boss was understanding, wanted to find out how to learn more, and what could be done to improve my skills and how I work. Working in a research centre my boss was supportive and would take the time to proof read my work.

At times at work I find reading slow (learning how to do something), I sometimes get to the point where I have to stop, re-read what I've already read or am unable to take in what I'm reading. Sometimes I'm easily distracted when reading. My work needs to proof read before it can be published (e.g. manuals). Writing documents / e-mails can take time especially when I'm proof reading and correcting.

I dislike organisation and admin and find that admin work takes time to do and can be distressing. I tend to worry about these tasks.

2.4 Maths in the Workplace

Steve Chinn

Difficulties that children have with maths are likely to persist into adulthood. This may, in part be due to the way it is taught.

Ofsted's last two reports on maths in schools commented on the dominant teaching style of relying on the recall of facts and procedures rather than on understanding. Whilst many people will forget what they tenuously learned at school, the impact of being taught to recall rather than to understand will have an even greater effect on most dyslexic learners.

Consequently many dyslexic workers will avoid doing maths in the workplace. This will have consequences for promotion as well as for coping with the mathematical demands of their current work.

There may also be an effect on self-esteem.

If a workplace is enlightened enough to offer training, this may well cause more anxiety than gratitude, especially if the training uses the methods that failed the worker when in school.

Whilst it is socially acceptable to admit, 'I could never do maths' without seemingly damaging self-esteem, that perceived inability can result in a person refusing to become involved in any training.

No involvement, no risk.

What Maths?

I have tried to construct a list to cover the topics that might constitute a maths programme/curriculum for the general workplace. I have checked this against the QCA Functional Skills Standards for Mathematics (www.qca.org.uk/functionalskills).

My list includes:

Money.

Time.

Timetables.

Measurement.

Estimation.

Graphs and pictorial presentation of information.

Percentages.

Computational skills.

Competent use of a calculator... and the ability to appraise the answer.

Probability.

The list is similar to the QCA curriculum, largely because the content is a logical and pragmatic summary of 'everyday' mathematics.

Of course, there are different levels of complexity for each of these topics. For example, money could cover working out a tip for a restaurant lunch, filling in an expenses claim or understanding a balance sheet.

I like the concept of learning what is necessary. This seems more sensible than presenting a learner with a programme that includes topics which, whilst defendable at an intellectual level, may create anxiety based rejection.

Dyslexia and Maths

Which of the topics above are likely to cause especial problems for dyslexic workers? What sub-skill deficits, for example working memory, will influence how easily people learn the topics?

There are three key underlying factors, short term/working memory, long term memory for maths facts and procedures and anxiety. There is an interaction between two of these which exacerbates their consequences and impact. Anxiety has a negative effect on working memory which in turn will have a negative effect on any maths, particularly any maths that is done 'mentally'.

There is research to suggest that dyslexics have great problems with the retrieval of some basic facts, especially if the retrieval has to be quick. (This problem, as with many of the problems discussed here, is not exclusive to dyslexics). The problem has several knock-on effects. For many it stirs memories of early failure in maths and thus creates anxiety and a sense of helplessness towards learning maths. It is possible to use strategies to access these facts, but there is a persistent belief that all people can simply learn the facts. Even in the QCA standards (Entry Level 3) there is 'use mental recall of multiplication tables 2, 3, 4, 5 and 10.' Most dyslexic learners can recall the facts for 2, 5 and 10, though even then the 2 and 5 facts are sometimes accessed by counting on. What is rarely explained is that, armed with these facts, it is possible to access all the other facts.

It is possible to substitute alternative, inter-linked, mutually supportive, dyslexia friendly procedures for standard procedures. These procedures are mathematical and understandable, but utilise the facts and knowledge that most dyslexic learners can access. Making the procedures and fact-accessing methods mutually supportive, aids recall and understanding. (The methods are explained in more detail in 'Dealing with Dyscalculia: Sum Hope 2.' Steve Chinn. Souvenir Press).

Calculators

Calculators can perform accurate computations, quickly, but they are not designed to think. If the data keyed in is wrong, then the answer will be wrong. Thus the provision of a calculator may not solve all the problems experienced by the worker.

There are a number of ways that entering data can be a problem. It could simply be a matter of hitting the wrong keys. Adding a long column of numbers would not be a relaxing activity and each step is an opportunity to make an error. It could be a matter of entering data in the order presented, for example, 30 ÷ 5 is presented in an order that works when used with a calculator. However, the order in 'Divide 5 into 30' does not work.

Estimation

The ability to estimate and to appraise answers is not natural for all learners. Estimation requires a different style of thinking to that needed for accurate computations. It also requires good number sense.

However, the ability to estimate is a life skill. Estimation requires a confidence with number values and the ability to inter-relate the four operations (+ - x ÷). It is a widely useful skill which is used in applications such as money, journey times, measurement and quantity.

If a worker does not have this skill, then it may be possible that accurate, procedure based calculations may suffice as an alternative, but this will only be effective if those calculations are consistently correct. Unfortunately that is not often the case.

There is, not surprisingly, a potential downside to having the skill of estimating. If it handicaps the ability to perform accurate calculations then, in some circumstances it may disadvantage a worker. This point illustrates a general aspect of employment: not all workers have all the skills. Employers can usually manage that situation.

Interpreting Data

There are occasions when information is presented mathematically, for example as a balance sheet or as a graph. It might be that the worker has to appraise the financial consequences of a percentage change in costs.

It can be hard for workers to admit to an intellectual weakness, so they may not ask the question that would clarify the information. Sometimes the presentation of that information will use technical jargon, or my own particular pet hate, acronyms that I don't recognise. It is difficult to process information and data if key facts and understanding are missing.

Anxiety

Unfortunately maths often creates anxiety. This anxiety is rarely facilitative. Indeed, it can create a total block to learning.

Issues around anxiety may well be the first area to address if a worker is being introduced to requirements that involve maths.

Of course, an adult has had many years to disguise the anxiety and its roots and consequences. Anxiety about new work centred on the perceived demands of the maths involved in a promotion or new job may well prevent the worker from applying for or accepting that job.

There is a 'maths anxiety in adults' questionnaire, with average scores on the website www.stevechinn.co.uk.

For further information on dyscalculia in adults, see 'Dealing with Dyscalculia' by Steve Chinn, Souvenir Press.

2.5 Perfect for Business - School Failure, Work Success

Thomas G. West

"I think a dyslexic personality is perfect for business.... If it doesn't take [a lot of book] study, if you can get [going] using your mouth or your feet, right from the beginning, my God, you are going to do well in business: you have a leg up...."

Barbara Corcoran is an entrepreneur, founder and former owner of a major real estate firm in New York City, The Corcoran Group, and author of the book Use What You've Got. She explains that she has long seen her own dyslexia as a great advantage in the world of business. She says you can always hire someone with the right kind of education who will be great with the banks. But she believes the traits that are really important to start and grow a business are the same traits that she has and many other dyslexics have: inventive marketing skills, intuitive management skills to develop staff loyalty, ability to conceive of a vision that will motivate and organize staff and joint venture partners. During an interview conducted in her offices in New York, she tells a story that is typical of the way she has learned to work, using her distinctive abilities (Corcoran, Creative Brains, 2005):

"I was always surprised when I was put into a room with a bunch of Harvard MBAs, well educated attorneys, all the A students, [who] would be working on some conceptual problem, some new direction, somewhere new we wanted to take the business or industry, and there were a lot of ideas in the room. But, to be honest with you, there were a lot of little ideas in the room. I had the ability to sit there like a sponge, kind of zone out on it, kind of get the little pieces, and come up with the big idea, each and every time. And more important than that, I could see how each person in the room was going to fit in a specific role in making it happen.... When I said it, 'Whoah, I've got it,' people learned to listen to me because I always got it. And most importantly, I could paint that big, bright picture, and everyone could see it... Nothing is better than giving a bunch of people running in different directions a roadmap that they all [could see] in living colour and it would motivate them and get them running off the page in the same direction. So, visualization and an ability to communicate are really the only two things that you need to [deal with] a bunch of disparate parts and make them a team.... If there is one thing that dyslexic people can very often do is make a bunch of people go left, right and in between: a big team buying into a big picture. But you have to be able to convey that picture."

In this passage, Corcoran sums up in a wonderfully informal and colourful way a perceptive insight into what may be one of the most important and distinctive characteristics shared by many dyslexics (within great diversity). When it comes to details, they may falter. They are not so good at remembering exactly what the teacher said or the exact argument used by this author or that. They may be a bit vague about the numbers cited or the lists of names given. However, sometimes, perhaps often, they can be very good at listening carefully and drinking in the whole situation in all its complexity; and slowly, quietly, working toward seeing a much larger integration of many diverse elements.

The "big picture" is an extraordinarily apt metaphor. We see it used so often - yet it tells us something of great importance. Corcoran can paint the "big, bright picture" "in living colour" to convey the vision that all can understand and be guided by.

She makes clear that those dyslexics who have this remarkable set of abilities, and there could be many, should be seen as perfectly well suited for the entrepreneurial side of business, that is, the most creative side.

Of course, they may have to rely on non-dyslexics to do much of the reading, research and detailed analysis that they find difficult or impossible. But, otherwise, they would appear to be well suited for positions where it is important to see the larger patterns, to see what others do not see, to see the world differently so they can find opportunities where others may see only problems and difficulties.

The world of entrepreneurial business, with so many opportunities, is also full of risk and uncertainty - requiring people who are able to learn from mistakes, those who are able to fall and pick themselves up again, wiser but with renewed conviction and energy. According to Corcoran, it would seem that dyslexic people (at least some of them, perhaps lots of them) are also remarkably well suited to the down side of entrepreneurial business as well:

"It really is easy to run and get the cup. The hard part is losing. ... What I think has been so helpful to me is that I spent all my early years losing. So, my God, how sweet the winning feels.... How easy it is to win. But a lot of people who have everything come easily, particularly the As and Bs in school, they don't know really what it feels like to lose. So it is pretty shocking when they get thrown out into the real world. For me, the more hits I took and the more failures I had, the more I felt at home."

Thomas G. West is the author of *In the Mind's Eye*, which deals with the talents of dyslexics and the way these talents have been used to make major contributions in various fields. He is also the author of *Thinking Like Einstein*, a compilation of articles written for professional computer graphic artists and technologists, a career path favoured by many dyslexics. After 15 printings, two translations (Japanese and Chinese), invited lectures in 14 countries and recognition as one of the "best of the best" for the year by the American Library Association, a second edition of In the Mind's Eye is to be released in September 2009.

References

Corcoran, Barbara, 2005. Transcribed from an interview in *Creative Brains; Gifted, Talented and Dyslexic*, a DVD dealing with "the other side of dyslexia, the creative side." Included are interviews with nine dyslexics: an entrepreneur, a restaurateur, a lawyer, two equestrian trainers, an advertising executive, an American Indian fashion designer, an author and an architect. Produced by Lois Rothschild and the Southwest Branch of the International Dyslexia Association. Directed by Tony Carlson. www.southwestida.com.

Corcoran, Barbara, with Bruce Littlefield, 2003. *Use What You've Got & Other Business Lessons I Learned from My Mom*. New York, NY: Portfolio, Penguin.

2.6 Workplace needs Assessments: How to Arrange and Appraise them

Sylvia Moody, Dyslexia in the Workplace,
British Dyslexia Association Organisational Member.

In this article I shall give advice on good practice in carrying out a workplace needs assessment (WNA) of dyslexia. I shall cover five topics:

1. What is the difference between a diagnostic assessment and a WNA?

2. What evidence is needed to do a WNA?

3. Who is qualified to do a WNA?

4. What should a WNA cover?

5. How should a WNA report be written?

In principle everything that is said in this article will apply also to assessment of other specific learning difficulties, e.g., dyspraxia, specific maths difficulty, attention deficit disorder.

I shall begin each section with what philosophers call an apophatic statement, that is a statement of what is not good practice, followed by a reported example of this. Then I shall give advice on what is good practice.

In general it may be said that bad practice results from one or more of the following:

■ The WNA is not comprehensive.

■ The assessor is not qualified to do WNAs specifically for dyslexia.

■ The WNA is conflated with a diagnostic assessment.

1. A workplace needs assessment is NOT a diagnostic assessment with a few recommendations tacked on

Jeremy, an educational psychologist, reports as follows:

I am sometimes asked by an HR or line manager to assess an employee who, they believe, may be dyslexic. I explain that the assessment is a two-phase operation, comprising a diagnostic assessment and a workplace needs assessment. However, some managers are unwilling to get involved in a more formal needs assessment and request that I just do a diagnostic assessment and provide some informal work-related recommendations. However, to me this always feels unprofessional and unsatisfactory.

Comment

To conflate a diagnostic assessment and a WNA, as described above, is not good practice. The two assessments each have a different focus; each will have a duration of two to three hours, and for the WNA the assessor usually travels to the client's workplace. So clearly a WNA cannot be reduced to a few paragraphs at the end of a diagnostic assessment.

Very occasionally the diagnostic assessor may decide that a WNA would be superfluous. An example is as follows:

Jack, a porter at a conference centre, was able to carry out his main portering duties without difficulty; however, he was occasionally called upon to cover for the receptionist and to take telephone messages. Because of his dyslexic difficulties he frequently made mistakes with these. As this was the only area of work in which he was inefficient, the diagnostic assessor felt it would be sufficient in this case to make an informal recommendation that Jack be offered a few sessions with a dyslexia tutor.

2. It is NOT wise to commission a WNA if a diagnostic assessment has not already been done

Jeremy again

Sometimes a client will come for a WNA without having had a diagnostic assessment. I had such a client recently, a 44-year-old man called John, who informed me only that he thought he might be 'a little bit dyslexic' as he had problems with writing. In a situation like this I am, frankly, floundering - I have so many unanswered questions: What is John's general intellectual level? What is his professional potential - is he aiming too high or too low? What are his strengths and talents? What is the nature and severity of his underlying difficulties? Is he 'a little bit dyslexic' or severely dyslexic? Is he perhaps also dyspraxic? Does he have attention deficit disorder or visual stress? What emotions have become tangled up with his basic difficulties through these not being recognised over a period of decades? How much would he be able to profit from a skills training programme? Without having the answers to these questions before me in the form of a diagnostic assessment report, I am really doing a needs 'guessment', not an assessment.

Comment

To this I only need to add my very strong recommendation that employers do commission a diagnostic assessment before proceeding to the workplace needs stage.

3. Chartered psychologists and dyslexia tutors are NOT automatically qualified to do workplace needs assessments

Jeannie, a line manager reports as follows:

We needed a workplace needs assessment for one of our employees, and contacted a large dyslexia organisation who recommended an assessor, an educational psychologist. When we received the psychologist's report of the assessment, we were surprised and disappointed that the recommendations had very little relevance to the difficulties that our employee was finding in her job. In fact some of them seemed more geared towards students than working people. The psychologist had recommended a tutor who could deliver relevant training, but - once bitten twice shy - I quizzed the tutor about his background, and it turned out that he had experience only in tutoring students, and had never tutored an employee.

Comment

The above situation arises quite frequently because most dyslexia professionals - psychologists and tutors - have been trained to work in an educational setting, and few have experience of supporting dyslexic people in the workplace. Occupational psychologists, of course, are fully conversant with a workplace culture, but they are not usually dyslexia specialists. Therefore, when searching for an assessor, the manager needs to check that the assessor has appropriate expertise and experience.

There are two ways of arranging a WNA, each of which has advantages and disadvantages. The first way is to arrange an assessment through the government's Access to Work scheme.

The advantage of this is that the assessment is provided free of charge, but possible disadvantages are that:

- the assessment may not be carried out by a dyslexia specialist.

- an individual workplace skills training programme (usually a crucial element in the support package) may not be specified.

- advice on appropriate adjustments to work requirements and/or workplace conditions may not be offered.

The second route is to go through a private dyslexia organisation which specialises in carrying out workplace needs assessments. The disadvantage of this route is that the employer (or the employee) has to fund the assessment, but the advantage is that the assessment will certainly be carried out by a dyslexia expert who will be able to make all the necessary recommendations.

Whichever route is chosen for the assessment, the employer can still apply to Access to Work for funding for the help required.

4. A workplace needs assessment for dyslexia is NOT an IT assessment

Duncan, a middle-ranking Civil Servant, reports as follows:

I was having some difficulties with my work: mainly time-management and general work organisation, and could not always express myself succinctly in meetings or when I was making presentations. My employers knew I had dyslexic and dyspraxic difficulties and were happy to arrange a workplace needs assessment for me. They found an assessor through a government scheme. When the assessor arrived, I explained my various difficulties to him, and he responded by suggesting a couple of items of software, one of which I was already using. When I asked him about some training to help with my dyspraxic problems, i.e. general organisation and communication abilities, he said he couldn't help me with this. In fact, it was clear to me that he was not quite sure what dyspraxia was. In his brief report on the 'assessment', he made no suggestions whatsoever for general skills training.

Comment

It is unfortunately the case that some organisations regard a WNA for dyslexia/dyspraxia as being essentially an IT assessment, and the assessors they provide may have little or no knowledge of the full range of dyslexic/dyspraxic difficulties or of the sort of skills training needed to alleviate these. In many jobs IT support is very helpful, but very rarely is it the whole answer.

So a WNA should include **all** of the following:

■ a summary of the client's strengths, difficulties and coping strategies as evidenced in the diagnostic report.

■ a consideration of any relevant emotional factors.

■ a detailed job description.

■ an explanation of how the client's difficulties affect his/her work efficiency.

■ detailed recommendations for a workplace skills training programme.

■ detailed recommendations for IT support.

■ advice on appropriate adjustments and any relevant legal issues.

■ suggestions for future monitoring of the client and liaison with the employer.

5. An assessment report should NOT be vague, jargony, speculative or over-long

Krishnan, a line manager reports as follows:

My main problem with psychologists' reports is that they are often very long and technical, and I have to work quite hard to understand the crucial points made in them. I just need a clear summary of the main difficulties and the measures we need to take to alleviate these. I want to know what training we need to put in and where we can find the relevant trainers.

Comment

It should be borne in mind that WNA reports are read by a number of people who are not dyslexia experts: Access to Work personnel, HR and line managers, occupational health advisers, and in some cases solicitors and barristers. It is, therefore, important that the report is clear, succinct and carefully structured. Technical data, costs of equipment and training, and general advice about dyslexia can all be put in appendices.

In the main body of the report **it is vital that the following three things are included:**

1. A detailed programme for workplace skills training. The programme should cover all aspects of literacy which are directly related to work - for instance, research skills, writing reports, reading technical manuals. General work skills should also be covered, e.g., dealing with job interviews or work reviews, contributing to meetings, understanding instructions, time-management, organisational skills. An initial training programme should ideally be around 30 hours spread over a period of at least three months.

2. Detailed recommendations for IT support, e.g., text-to-speech and concept mapping software. Advice should also be given here about how the IT training can be delivered in a dyslexia-friendly manner.

3. Recommendations for appropriate adjustments at both the individual and the organisational level.

If the WNA report does **not** include all these, then the relevant manager should take the matter up with the assessor, or with the organisation that has provided the assessor, and request relevant additions to the recommendations. If necessary, a second, more comprehensive, WNA should be carried out by a more qualified assessor.

Further Reading

Dyslexia and Employment: A Guide for Assessors, Trainers and Managers. Edited by Sylvia Moody. Wiley-Blackwell 2009.

Chapter 3: How to do a workplace needs assessment.

Chapter 6: How to do an assistive technology assessment.

Chapter 9: How to deliver a skills training programme.

Information point B: Reasonable adjustments.

2.7 Case Study
Professor Paul Palmer, Cass Business School

Professor Palmer says: "My mum realised I wasn't going to get the support I needed in the state system. She and my dad worked very hard to be able to pay for me to go to private school, where the smaller classes were of benefit to me." Paul also received extra tuition for his English and spelling. It was during this time that Paul caught up with his peers and passed his 11 plus, after which he went to the local comprehensive school.

Paul worked for many charities and not-for-profit organisations, including a housing project for young people and a national drug rehabilitation centre. He worked his way up the career ladder with his extensive knowledge of charity financial, management and governance issues, and as a qualified chartered company secretary, he took a place at South Bank University as head of the finance division. Paul was then funded to do a PhD on External Regulation and Internal Control in the Charity Sector, which became a 137,000-word volume of work over two large books. In between all this Paul has even found the time to write five books.

Paul is openly transparent about his dyslexia and although it has not prevented him from succeeding in his chosen career, he does still find it a problem: "It is a constant fight. I was able to write my PhD due to the advent of the word processor, but it wouldn't have happened without that."

"I am increasingly still frustrated and annoyed that people, particularly some politicians and business leaders express uninformed and hurtful remarks about dyslexia. These comments remind me of the views that were expressed some 150 years to John Stuart Mill when he published his paper on women's suffrage. Similarly, the recent election in the US of Barack Obama has clearly laid to dust those wicked opinions that used to be expressed about black people and intelligence. As these two issues highlight the forces of reactionary ignorance can be overcome. I hope that in the next few years we will see the same reform to those opinions about dyslexia."

3. Using Technology

3.1 What's hot in technology?

Ian Smythe

Technology is not the solution, but it can be part of a strategy that helps reduce difficulties. At the end of 2008, I made a list on my blog (http://technodys.blogspot.com) of what I considered to be some of the most useful software around. Here are the highlights from that list, and a reason why I would recommend them to anybody. (For fuller details, see the blog entry of 1st January 2009.) And it is all free!

Firstly, My Top Three for 2008 were:

1. SearchMe
2. DimDim
3. Soshiku

SearchMe - Do you hate when you have to read all those entries in Google? Would you like to see the websites visually? Then this is the search engine for you - www.searchme.com

Dimdim - There is nothing worse than trying to get some software support as they shout down the phone "No, it should not be like that. Try the other one!" Dimdim is described as web conferencing. It allows voice and video, text chat, and most importantly, a shared deskspace where somebody can look at your working environment - www.dimdim.com

Soshiku - This is an online reminder system. There are many others, but I like the ease of use of this one. You can set it to send emails and text messages ahead of assignment and project deadlines - www.soshiku.com

Others of note were as follows:

KeePass - This is probably my most used piece of software on this list. I keep all my passwords here in one place, so all I have to do is remember the one password to enter it - www.keepass.com

iSpeech - Simply upload your text document to this site, and you can download the mp3 file. You can also enter a URL or text - www.ispeech.org

IM Translator - This is a wonderful online tool which translates (and back translates) in more than a dozen languages, and with the text being spoken by avatars - http://imtranslator.com

Raptor - Plagiarism is wrong. But accidental plagiarism is a real danger when you are trying to track multiple sources. This software will compare your text with what is on the web and highlight where there is common text - www.scanmyessay.com

Mindmeister - This online collaborative concept mapping tool allows team work over distance. Free for a limited number of concept maps - www.mindmeister.com

Reading Survey - This website allows you to identify your preferences for background colour, typeface, font size etc. - www.wdnf.info/colours/en/

Zhorn Stickies - These desktop stickies (desktop visual reminders) continue to be my favourites, despite others arriving on the scene. They also include alarms - www.zhornsoftware.co.uk/stickies/

Dropbox - There is nothing worse than suddenly not having access to information because your computer died. This site provides online storage, and allows you to set the back-up to be done automatically. - www.getdropbox.com

There were also a couple of highlights which do not fall into the free category, but are worth highlighting for their innovation. The first is the ability to enter text into your concept map (currently only MindManager) using speech-to-text, and the other was to use an iPhone to search the web.

3.2 Network Solutions

Dave Evans, Microlink PC, British Dyslexia Association New Technologies Committee

Historically, the treatment of dyslexia in the workplace has been compliance driven and inseparable from the Reasonable Adjustment (RA) process. However, as the more savvy parts of the Human Resource community learn more about the nature, scale and incidence of the condition, it is finally being treated as just another component of talent management, and the technological solutions therefore as productivity tools. With this has come a more proactive stance which is having a surprising impact on the non dyslexic workforce.

It is not surprising that HR managers remain fearful of the compliance agenda set by the Disability Discrimination Act (DDA) and, in the Public Sector, the Disability Equality Duty (DED) and it is worth reflecting on the significance of this legislative framework for dyslexics.

Any HR manager will know that the DDA imposes an obligation to make 'reasonable adjustments' to the working environment of a disabled person and that this duty can be discharged in most cases through the frequently laborious Access to Work scheme, but fewer would really understand what 'reasonable' really means in this context. The standard Common Law definition of what is reasonable is ascribed to the opinion of 'the man on the Clapham omnibus', but this generic definition doesn't help much in making sense of dyslexia based reasonable adjustments. What should be remembered is that the determination of what is reasonable is the prerogative of a High Court Judge looking over a case with the benefit of hindsight and may therefore be based on three key questions:

What information was available in the public domain about the condition at the time? *i.e. should the HR manager have known about it?*

How effective might we expect an adjustment to be? *(i.e. is the adjustment likely to make a difference?)*

Is the cost proportionate to the benefit and therefore *'reasonable'?*

In the context of dyslexia the questions can be answered quickly and compellingly. It wouldn't take a Judge long on Google to find dozens, probably hundreds, of credible academic research papers suggesting that perhaps 1 in 10 people could be identified on a dyslexic spectrum. Indeed, a quick visit to the British Dyslexia Association website would produce the same result. It wouldn't take them much longer to find a further body of evidence to suggest that technological interventions make a massive difference to working lives of most dyslexics. In a recent telephone poll conducted by MicrolinkPC, over 80% of people who had received technological support believed that their performance had improved, and over 70% said that they use the technology on a daily basis. The sector does need more scientific research on this, but there is enough persuasive findings already out there to say that interventions work.

So in simple terms, a HR manager should have known that up to 10% of their staff will be dyslexic and that the provision of technological support would make a big difference to their working conditions. This alone does not compel an employer to act - the cost of an adjustment must also be proportionate and not prohibitively expensive to warrant being 'reasonable'. So how much does the technology cost? This depends on the individual case but we believe it should normally be less than 1% of total employment cost (based on an average salary and

3 year adjustment cycle). These are pretty compelling figures and woe betide any HR manager forced to defend themselves for non-compliance in an industrial tribunal or Court of Law.

Furthermore, given that damages for successful discrimination cases are un-capped, it is far more practical to be proactive and support dyslexics with readily available adjustments.

Despite the compelling case for reasonable adjustments made above, Dr Nasser Siabi, founder and MD of MicrolinkPC (the country's largest independent supplier of assistive technology), argues focussing on the compliance debate 'misses the point'. He believes that a proactive stance on dyslexia will not only be cost effective but will benefit a huge hidden population of people with literacy challenges at work. *"Why should I wait for staff to ask for dyslexia support before I provide it when I know that they will be more productive and much happier with it?'* This question goes to the heart of the dyslexia at work debate.

Whilst many people have benefited significantly from the Access to Work scheme it remains an essentially reactive system which places both psychological and bureaucratic barriers in the way of productive work practices, which usually means that only the most extreme cases or persistent applicants are dealt with, which in turn means that the vast majority of dyslexics go unrecognised. This should be an even greater driver for HR managers to act to counter the threat of the compliance stick because it has a direct impact on productivity and human asset management. Put simply, if you know that 10% of your workforce are likely to have some form of dyslexia and your RA procedures have picked up say just 2%, how much more productive would the remaining 8% be if they were given some technological support and training?

At the time of going to press there are several pilot projects underway which have run mainstream dyslexia support software programs across company networks and made them available to all staff. The results are still being measured but initial feedback is impressive. We are finding as many as 28% are using one or more of the programs available on a regular basis. Perhaps this should be expected, as many jobs now require a far higher degree of text literacy than in the past and many people with moderate problems are asking for help. At a recent dyslexia workshop at the regional headquarters of one of the country's leading banks, a female member of staff described to me how she had always found dealing with words a little difficult but thought that she had become more dyslexic with age. She had started work as a clerk and had worked her way up the career ladder. I accompanied her to her workstation to find three computer monitors with no fewer than five live data feeds plus her own work open. She had two phones on her desk and was working in a noisy office environment. Small wonder that she was struggling to cope! She (like many others) would never appear on a dyslexia register or sign up for a reasonable adjustment, but has benefited enormously from the availability of *text-to-speech* and *speech-to-text* technology available on the network. An exact measure of the impact on her productivity, motivation and engagement of her work would be difficult to measure, but certainly it is very positive.

Naysayers would argue that providing network solutions is overkill and prohibitively expensive. Not so! Central procurement is massively more cost effective than buying individual copies of software. For example, an enterprise copy of Dragon 10 Professional cost about £600; and for Claro Read (an outstanding text-to-speech reader about £200, for an individual user, but an annual network wide licence for both would cost from £10,000. So with new thinking come new efficiencies and new ways of looking at software procurement. As the dual effects of the increasingly powerful diversity lobby and the financial realities of the credit crunch bite we see real opportunities for empowering more workers and saving precious resources at the same time.

For more information email corporatesolutions@microlinkpc.com

3.3 Using Text to Speech to Support Reading and Writing in the Workplace

Sally McKeown (Becta) and Dave Stevens
(Claro Software, British Dyslexia Association
Organisational Member).

These days, it's almost impossible to find a job which does not involve reading and writing. Take the assistant who changes your tyre in the garage and then has to enter your details on a database and print out the invoice, or what about the decorator who sends you an estimate for redecorating your living room? They both need to be able to turn out well presented, correctly spelt text that makes sense. They may also need to improve their reading skills as Andy explains:

"My job as a tiler is literally very hands on but recently I got a request to clean up a Minton tiled floor. Now my reading is pretty slow and I find it hard to get information from books. I didn't want to get it wrong because the floor was over a hundred years old so I knew I would have to check it out. I used a screen reader with text to speech technology, alongside Google, and read up about Minton. In the end, I contacted a couple of companies that specialise in this kind of work. Because the screen reader had helped me to 'read up' about problems with the porosity of different coloured tiles, I was able to talk quite confidently and ask the right questions."

There are a number of text to speech programs (also sometimes called screen readers) that will read out text highlighted on screen or selected by the mouse and copied to the clip board. This can be very good news for people who have reading difficulties or dyslexia or who just need to give their eyes a rest.

At a simple level there is Windows' Narrator but this is not designed to read back large chunks of text in a document or a web page.

In fact, more refined programs such as ClaroRead would let Andy listen to any text underneath the mouse cursor, by using a human quality voice to speak that text. He could also scan pages from technical manuals into Microsoft Word, put the cursor at the beginning of the text he wanted to hear, press the ClaroRead Play button and sit back and listen to the information. He could even type in his own comments, click on the Save as Audio button, choose a suitable destination on his computer and have all the text saved as a sound file.

Help with Writing

Technology can also help with writing both at the composing and proof reading stages. Some people like to produce a complete rough draft and then listen to it but those with poor short term-memory or concentration difficulties may prefer to have text read back as they type. Screen readers can also help with proof reading. It is especially useful for people who confuse the letters b and d since they will often hear the difference when the word is read out. Speech can also help in those cases where someone has typed in the wrong word as in the sentence, 'Humphrey Bogart stared in Casablanca.' Since stared is correctly spelt, it would not be picked up by a spell checker but the writer can hear that it is wrong. It can also highlight repetitious phrasing as Laura discovered:

"I wrote about my job for a blog and then decided to listen to it. When the text was read back, I knew I would have to change the wording. I think I might have realised that I had over-used the word 'hotel' but I was not aware that I'd written 'now' three times."

Ways of Supporting Employees

Is your induction handbook available electronically? There's no point having essential documents available just as printed text as it will not help employees who are not good readers. If it is available electronically, it can be used with a screen reader and headphones and even better, it will be searchable: no more flicking through pages looking for the section on annual leave arrangements.

Send out the agenda for meetings in advance, in electronic format, and make sure minutes are available on the company intranet and emailed as well.

Explore the idea of adding narration to existing resources.

Office software such as Microsoft Word and Microsoft PowerPoint will support sound clips. Instead of just looking at a dull PowerPoint with lots of text in different fonts with clip art embellishments, viewers can listen to a narrative and get a real sense of the purpose of the presentation. Narration is also a useful aid for people who are poor public speakers. Be warned though, narration does create larger file sizes. Think about using audio files for 'verbal notes'. Audacity is a free audio editor and recorder which can record live audio via a microphone or import audio from another source, such as the audio component of a training video. The clips can be edited and then saved as audio files for the staff to download and use on their portable players.

Think about how you use PDFs. This file format is very useful and provides access to lots of hard copy materials such as manuals, publicity, information leaflets etc. Properly constructed, PDFs can be very accessible to a wide range of users. If badly made, they are a nightmare. TechDis recently conducted a survey of the online prospectuses put out by colleges as a marketing tool and reported, 'Adobe Acrobat uses a computerised voice to read the pages.

In general, when the text is formatted in a simplistic way the tool worked well. However, when text boxes are used, the reading order can sometimes get confused. Also having tables within the literature can be very difficult for somebody using this function to understand.'

Finally, a story to show that the timely use of technology can make an appreciable difference. Rod was employed as a temp in a purchasing department. He got on well with his colleagues but his line manager was irritated by what she saw as his careless writing. Rod frequently omitted words from letters and emails which made them impossible to understand. Even more importantly, despite using a spreadsheet, his calculations were inaccurate as he transposed numbers and put decimal points in the wrong place. Fortunately one of his colleagues suspected that Rod might have dyslexia and arranged for him to talk to his union representative and a human resources manager. Rod was given a screen reader that read back the numbers as he typed them. As he had good estimation and numerical reasoning skills, he learnt how to compensate for his poor proof reading. He has recently been offered a permanent job.

Most screen readers and text to speech software programs are available on a trial basis, so it is a good idea to try some out to see if they are helpful.

The Access to Work Scheme (www.direct.gov.uk) can help people like Rod. Financial assistance may be available to provide technology, guidance and training to support anyone whose health or disability affects the way they do their job.

Claro Software Ltd is a UK assistive software company providing high quality, easy to use software to benefit computer users with reading difficulties and sight problems. www.clarosoftware.com.

ClaroRead SE is available for trial via www.clarosoftware.com/bda.

3.4 Case Study

Jason Crandley, Artist

I don't recall a lot about my school days as a young boy, but I recall being tested for dyslexia between 6-8. It was not until my teens that I started to think about the reading and spelling. I tried my hand at music to hide from the dyslexia but I found I was not good at that. Woodwork was something I was good at, not reading or spelling.

When I was about to leave school, I was asked if I would like to go to art college, but I felt it wasn't for me, I didn't want any more school or spelling books. To this date I wish I had gone, but going through life with dyslexia had its pitfalls, like now I have to look for some kind of work, but I look for jobs where I could use my hands and not my brain.

I don't know how I got this far in life, as no matter where I looked you had to read things and fill out forms. But the big thing I found hard was remembering things, I could find ways round the reading and spelling.

I am not too sure when art came in to my life but it has always been hiding away, just coming out now and then. It was not until my mid 20s that I started painting more and more.

My reading got better, thanks to my mum, as she would give me books to read, and now I am a bit of a bookworm. That has also help with form filling, so in a way I have over come the dyslexia from the reading part of it. I taught myself how to paint and draw, I now use it as a way out and feel that putting the paint on the canvas is like putting words down on paper, sometimes I don't have to think about it.

My breakthrough came in 2003 when I put on my first Exhibition selling my art and I am now a full time artist. I am happy that I have made it this far in life, being dyslexic does not mean you can't do it, it just means it will take you longer to do something, and I may forget some things but in time I will get there.

3.5 Assistive Technology for the Workplace
EA Draffan

Discussing the subject of assistive or helpful technology in the workplace is rather like buying a pair of shoes for someone you have never met. You might suggest the wrong type of shoes for the job, an incorrect fit, something that turns out to be uncomfortable to use, or perhaps worst of all, does not suit the individual's personal preferences. So whether you are wanting to use technology when you are working or are supporting someone else in their use of technology it is important to explore the:

- type of environment in which the technologies will be used,

- access to assistive technologies,

- skills and abilities of the user and personal preferences,

- different assistive technologies on offer,

- likely ongoing support, training and reviews.

Working Environment

The type of technologies chosen will depend on the work environment. The range is enormous from working with a computer, working with people, on the move all day, outside, commercial, education, government, health, leisure or sports industries to name but a few. There will be the issues of remote working and connectivity along with the types of computers in the workplace compared to those at home, such as Apple Mac and Windows PCs or Linux. If handheld devices are to be used, these may need to be synchronised with computer operating systems or linking to the office network for updating appointments, e-mail and access to the intranet and web.

One way of establishing the pros and cons for using various types of technologies is to list the important tasks taking place each working day and then those that are important but only occur at regular intervals, such as updating a time sheet or claiming expenses.

Access to Technologies

When discussing access to different types of technologies, this may be linked to the cost of the technologies - whether this is a personal purchase of equipment, supported by Access to Work (http://tinyurl.com/3b3m7w) and the employer or provided by other work schemes or charity. There are often free alternatives but they are rarely available across networks or have the training support.

A problem that is more likely to arise is the lack of ease with which assistive technologies can be used on work computers, either across a network or on an individual work station, due to the permissions or security measures in place.

Being unable to access the desktop properties on a computer may mean that the accessibility options that are bundled with an operating system may also be unobtainable, so colour changes, text to speech and magnification cannot be implemented or the look and feel of the desktop icons, folders etc cannot be changed.

It may be that certain software, such as speech recognition (where one is dictating into the computer and the text appears on the screen) is unavailable on the network or voice files cannot be stored. Some of these problems can be solved by the use of specialist software being carried on Pen Drives or Universal Serial Bus (USB) Flash Memory Sticks. But once again, if access to the computer's USB ports/connections is not allowed, as is the case in some organisations due to the nature of the work being carried out, there may be difficulties using for example text to speech software for reading out data and highlighting text.

Skills, Abilities and Preferences

Assessing where strengths and weakness lie in the use of technology is not always easy, especially if it involves tasks that have always caused concern, for example reading from the screen or paper, writing long reports, making notes in meetings, or recording items said in a phone conversation or out on-site.

Noting down personal preferences in the same way as tasks is important. This often reveals where strengths lie and how one can work through these abilities to support aspects of work that are harder to accomplish. For example, it may be much easier to discuss items of importance and capture someone's imagination with a drawing or mind map rather than providing a list or handout for a presentation.

Assistive Technologies

Reading from the Screen or Paper

If reading from any screen is difficult then having the text read with a synthesised voice may help; but if the voice sounds annoying, turn it off and just use the word or phrase highlighting available with some software (Texthelp Read & Write and ClaroRead).

Handhelds and mobile phones can also be equipped with this type of software (CapturaTalk). Form Pilot may also help when it comes to reading and filling in forms. A virtual Screen Ruler (Claro Software) can help to keep the eyes on track when working on long documents or highlighting particular points in a presentation.

Changing the colour of text or the background may be one of the easiest options or even the whole screen (ClaroView) if visual stress or the glare of black on white is an issue. Font size and the gap between lines or words can also be changed in most word processors to help with reading.

For documents only available on paper, scanning and using optical character recognition (OCR) (Abby Fine Reader, OmniPage Pro or TextHelp and Claro software) to convert them into accessible digital format may be an option, but it takes time. Once on the computer or hand held reading pen they can be read aloud or the text highlighted. Photocopying to make the text bigger or a change to coloured paper may help, as can coloured acetate overlays to dull the glare of black text on white background. Handwriting can often cause the most problems: asking for items to be typed may be the only option. Handheld pen scanners or larger document scanning can usually save the text, but normally as a picture because OCR is not very successful at transcribing handwriting into editable text.

Writing and Note Taking

Planning may not be a strength, but drawing or using mind maps (Inspiration, Mind Genius, Mind Manager) can be very useful for generating ideas and this type of software is available both on the computer and on websites for free (MindMeister).

Whilst composing documents or making notes and even sending e-mails, having the text read aloud for checking spelling and sentence construction usually works well. Even if the voice is annoying, (although it should be noted that the voices have improved enormously), the fact a word is said in an odd way can often highlight an error.

Most word processors offer spell checking with or without a grammar check, but this does not always guarantee that all mistakes will be corrected. It can be helpful to have an electronic dictionary (Franklin spell checker) or access to Google to check complex or unusual words. You can often spot the correct spelling, as Google will provide a phrase somewhere in the search results or offer an alternative at the outset. Dictionary.com can also be useful if you are online.

If typing is not a strength and nor is composing text then speech recognition (Dragon NaturallySpeaking or MacSpeech Dictate) can help but there is a learning curve involved and it is not easy to use in a busy open plan office or when on the road. Dictating notes into a recorder and having them typed up later is another option or even dictating and hoping your voice is clear enough for it to be transcribed later with speech recognition is a possibility. Locator dots on the computer keyboard or coloured key cap labels can help with typing. If copying text or numbers is an issue, using two screens adds extra desktop space for electronic documents or using a copyholder with a slide ruler for paper based documents.

Organisation Skills and Time Management

Most mobile phones and PDAs synchronise with computers allowing for the matching up of appointments, task lists, contacts and many other files and folders that may be available on a work intranet. They generally have small recorders for instant notes along with alarms for reminders. It is also worth remembering sticky coloured notes and coloured felt tip pens or highlighters as low tech reminders! Not all technology needs to be complex and the watch with timer can also be useful.

Ongoing Support

Keep technology simple as ongoing support often disappears over time, as does the chance of renewing assistive technology. Ideally making friends with the technology support team should be a long term aim, as not all technologies are specialist and many changes can be achieved with the software already available on most workstations. There are also many freely available applications that can be downloaded, but permissions may need to be granted.

All the Windows technologies mentioned in this article (other than speech recognition), are available on a pen drive, so can be used when hot desking or moving between sites.

Resources

It has not been possible to cover all aspects of the use of Assistive Technologies for the workplace, but the BDA has an Employer's Guide to Dyslexia: www.bdadyslexia.org.uk/news28.

Also a web page listing 'Reasonable Adjustments in the Workplace': www.bdadyslexia.org.uk/adjustments, plus links to the technologies mentioned in this article: www.bdastore.org.uk and a list of freely available software: www.bdadyslexia.org.uk/aboutdyslexia69.

3.6 AdysTrain - Supporting Dyslexics in the European Workforce

Bernadette Frech and Thomas Schmalzer

FH JOANNEUM, University of Applied Sciences
Department of International Management
Graz, Austria

Dyslexia is not a problem that restricts itself to the English language. The problems are universal, though the manifestation may differ in each language. Experts estimate that up to 25 million workers in Europe are affected by dyslexia, and while there is reasonable knowledge in the UK and an increasing level of support, this is not the case across Europe. The lack of awareness and understanding, as well as the means to support, means that the disability laws are largely ignored in many countries.

Against this background, an international project group came together under AdysTrain in 2005 with the aim to contribute to the creation of awareness and understanding of dyslexia in adulthood. The two-year project was funded by the European Commission, and was a collaboration between Austria, Bulgaria, Denmark, Finland and Germany Hungary, Spain and the UK. It included experts in dyslexia, e-learning, training and technology.

The main objectives of the project were

1) Helping employers become aware of dyslexia and how it may affect their workforce. The interactive information was designed to help employers to address the needs of dyslexic people by making them aware of the "reasonable adjustments" they may need to make, particularly in relation to workplace training, as well as indicating what benefits dyslexic people may bring to the workplace. The interactive course helped dispel myths about dyslexia, indicate how dyslexia may affect adults at work, and help employers to consider how dyslexia may affect their colleagues and customers.

2) Assisting workplace trainers and those organizing training to consider how they can make sure their practices are "dyslexia friendly". It included guidance on producing training materials and training methods.

The principal output was an e-book, designed to help trainers and employers in the following areas:

- What is dyslexia?

- Identification of the strengths and weaknesses of dyslexic individuals

- Underlying causes of dyslexia

- Information and Communication Technology (ICT)

- Learner preferences and learning styles

- The dyslexic learner

- Materials for the dyslexic learner

- Multilingualism and dyslexia

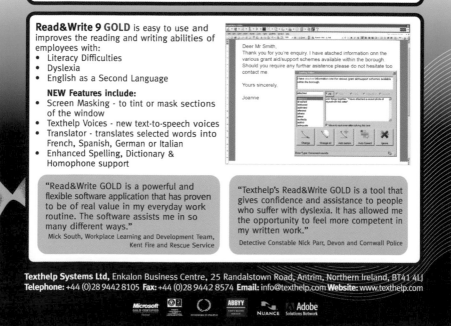

Your perfect pocket companion

DS-65 Digital Recorder.
High-quality audio processing at your fingertips.

The DS-65 is incredibly easy to navigate with its tactile buttons and optional voice guidance system, which enables audible navigation through menus and instant voice information on the battery level. The zoom microphone function allows you to record by focusing on sound from any direction. All this makes the capture and review of dictations, meetings and personal notes a breeze. In addition to high-quality recording and playback of WMA files, the large 2GB storage capacity enables you to listen to MP3 and audible content files.

So however long your day and wherever it takes you, you can count on the DS-65 to keep you efficient and entertained.

www.olympus.co.uk

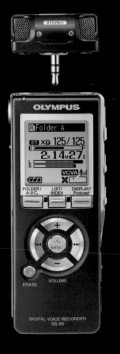

DS YOUR LIFE ®

- Disseminating good practice and career guidance

- Self-awareness and self-advocacy groups

- Dyslexia and disability legislation

In order to ensure quality, pilot projects were set up in each country with respect to not only the manuals listed above but also the training that was given in association with the manuals.

This Pilot Phase was a crucial stage of the process, and one that many organisations should consider when preparing material. Despite the content being written by leading experts, there was still valuable input from course participants that led to a more dyslexia-friendly product, and one that helped the target audience of employers, entrepreneurs, trainers, and lecturers throughout Europe to discover the hidden potential of their dyslexic employees and learners.

www.adystrain.org

3.7 Towards a Corporate Policy on Accessible Format Materials

Ian Litterick, Iansyst and British Dyslexia Association New Technology Committee and Organisational Member.

Since December 2006, there has been a legal duty on all public sector organisations to promote equality of opportunity for disabled people, the Disability Equality Duty or DED. This brings an obligation to produce a Disability Equality Scheme or DES. Your DES will usually say that you will make written information available in alternative accessible formats for those with reading difficulties.

Whilst Private Sector Organisations do not have such a specific duty, you do have obligations under the Disability Discrimination Acts and it is good Corporate Social Responsibility policy to think proactively about how you make information available to reading impaired people whether they are visually impaired, dyslexic or have other cognitive or physical difficulties.

This article discusses the steps you should take to:

■ Communicate your organisation's messages effectively

i. to reading impaired staff, customers and other stakeholders;

ii. whilst minimising costs in origination, administration and distribution of accessible format materials.

What are reasonable adjustments to help with reading? What formats are accessible to people with reading impairments?

Many dyslexic people also suffer from Visual Stress, also known as Meares-Irlen syndrome and various other names. They have difficulty focussing and moving their eyes in coordinated jumps to track words ("saccades"), such that the print may appear to move, swim or blur. (They may not realise that it doesn't do this for everybody!) Their needs are similar to those of partially sighted people. They may benefit from:

1. Changing font size and style;

2. Changing foreground and background colours;

3. Changing the spacing between characters, words and lines;

4. Being able to listen to the text using a screen reader with a Text to Speech (TTS) synthesiser.

Dyslexic people who have difficulties decoding the words of the text and blind people who cannot see it at all will also benefit from being able to listen to the text.

You can most easily provide for all these needs with a suitable electronic version of the text. Then, where people have the appropriate technology, they can use it to change the text to suit them, or to listen to it.

With longer electronic documents you also need to have structure - e.g. a table of contents where you can click on a chapter to go there. This is useful for anyone, but particularly important for blind people who can't skim a document and look at page numbers easily.

In addition you may need to provide easy read versions (abbreviated and simplified) of some documents for people with general learning difficulties. In any case you should always make sure that documents are in Plain English as that is easier and clearer for everyone to read and usually shorter.

You will then only rarely be asked to provide documents in Braille, hard copy for large print etc, or audio files. People will usually prefer a document that they can get to now, e.g. over the web or intranet, rather than having to wait for someone to send it.

1) Avoid as far as possible having to provide documents in alternative formats: make them accessible in the first place as routine

Try to avoid having to make documents accessible after they are finished. "Post-Hoc Accessifying" (PHA) of documents is almost always:

- Time-consuming;

- Expensive;

- Inefficient;

- Too late;

- So inconvenient that people mostly won't ask for them (thank heavens, given the expense!);

- and liable to be wrong as the accessifier doesn't know the subject as well as the author does.

So:

2) Try to work accessibility into your document creation process

This is not as easy as it could be. A start is to use Microsoft Word's more efficient Styles rather than using the typical hodgepodge of ad hoc formatting that many of us do. Styles should be a normal part of enforcing corporate presentation standards. By using styles for headings, bullets etc you have already built basic navigation into your document, because you can automatically generate a table of contents that links back to each section.

Authors need some (not much!) training to produce accessible documents. It would be better if word processors like Word provided **Incidental Obligatory Accessibility**, if they always asked the right questions and discouraged the wrong type of formatting, so that you wrote accessibly without trying and without needing to be skilful.

For example, to meet the needs of blind people all images need to have "alt text" with them, to describe the image if it is meaningful, or to remain empty if the image is purely decorative. Tables need rows and columns labelling, so that people relying on screen readers can hear to identify each cell.

If authors can learn to do these things for themselves, then it takes little extra time - even less when the software prompts properly - and the author controls the content themselves.

3) **If possible use Microsoft Word or html as your output format, rather than PDF**

Publishers and designers like PDF (Portable Document Format) because they can make an electronic document for people to read on a computer, but which looks exactly like it did on paper. They have full and detailed control of what can be quite complex formatting. They can also have control of copying and printing and even apply sophisticated Digital Rights Management (DRM) to it if they wish. Many of these controls can make it difficult or impossible for the computer to read the text out loud - depending on the sophistication and expense of the screenreader software on the one hand and the skill of the user on the other.

Above all publishers like PDFs because they probably sent the document to the printer as a PDF, so they can publish an electronic version extremely easily, on the web for example, almost as a by-product.

It is possible to make PDFs accessible, but it is not easy.

Typesetting is often subcontracted to people who are not concerned about the accessibility of the electronic version, so accessibility is often dire unless it is expressly demanded. We won't go into detail here as to how to make a PDF accessible. Adobe publish a series of documents telling you how to do it. You can produce accessible PDFs with Adobe's own InDesign publishing program, but it is impossible with the rival Quark Express. Even accessible PDFs are very difficult to read on mobile phones, where the reading software is less well developed. As mobile phones increasingly become the universal device of choice, people will increasingly expect to be able to do this.

Word, on the other hand produces accessible documents comparatively easily and you can read them with a screen reader without problems. Web pages in html are also comparatively easy to produce accessibly and to read with assistive technology. There are free tools that check your pages automatically and help guide you as to how accessible they are. (But you still need a human tester as well).

4) If you have to use PDFs - some things to check

You can create three types of PDF file, which at first sight all look the same:

- Image;

- Searchable image;

- Formatted text and graphics.

Image PDFs are rare on the web - fortunately so, because they are a pain. They are usually created by scanning pages of text and just contain an image of the text not the separate characters and words of the text itself. So most screen readers cannot read them as they are.

Searchable image files are better because they have a copy of the actual text behind the image. So screen readers can read the text and search engines like Google can index these files.

But it is formatted text and graphics that you need if the file is to be truly accessible.

In addition to navigation structure and image labels, PDFs, which can have complex formatting and boxes, need tagging to show a reading order for screen readers to follow.

Finally, avoid restricting the use that people can make of your documents - see the attached illustration of Adobe Reader's Properties/Security tab. Some people may like to do so for copyright and other reasons. But whilst some of the more expensive screen readers can read practically anything, many readers will be locked out if you impose copying restrictions. Mobiles, Macs and cheaper and free assistive technology may not be able to read PDFs if copying is not allowed.

Ian Litterick is Executive Chairman of Iansyst Ltd (www.iansyst.co.uk), a member of the BDA New Technologies Committee and an associate member of the Right to Read Campaign. A version of this chapter, with links, will be regularly updated at www.re-adjust.co.uk/alt-format-policy and will link to more detailed resources on accessible formats and on tools and techniques to make best use of documents however accessible they are.

3.8 Case Study

Cara Cramp, Specialist Teaching Assistant

Having dyslexia is frustrating. You know what you want to say but it takes you ages to write it because you have to think so hard about the order of the words and letters and then you've got to remember punctuation and grammar.

When I was little I was good at remembering word shapes so when it came to reading books I read them from memory. By the time I was at middle school I hated reading, until I discovered the strategy of reading the first and last page and the synopsis at the back of the book. I'd learnt that the teacher only ever asked you what the book was about and how it ended so if I could remember the plot and the characters I was on to a winner and it worked.

In 2000 I worked as a Community Nursery Nurse. I coped ok for two years; I had strategies in place to enable me to do my job effectively. Strategies I used unconsciously. Then my job changed. All of a sudden I was asked to work across two bases and that meant implementing two ways of working. I started to struggle. I had a colleague whose teenage son was going through assessment for dyslexia and she talked about his difficulties.

I arranged to have a formal dyslexia assessment by an Educational Psychologist. The report concluded that I did indeed have dyslexia. I felt relieved but also embarrassed and didn't want anyone to know.

It's been 5 years now since my assessment and in that time I have been to college and learnt some more strategies to improve my reading. I have also achieved my adult teaching certificate in further education. I am now a Specialist Teaching Assistant working with Primary aged children in different schools, supporting them with their individual learning needs.

It's taken me a long time to be able to tell people that I work with about having dyslexia because people at work assume things. They focus on the reading and writing aspect of dyslexia and forget about the secondary difficulties like poor sequential working memory.

I'm involved with my Local Dyslexia Association. Being involved with the BDA has helped me to become more open about dyslexia. I know that when I am there people will value my input and not laugh or become impatient when I am having a 'dyslexic moment', of which I'm sure everyone can relate to, even those who say they are not dyslexic!

3.9 Speech-to-text: Putting Together the Right Solution

Peter Kelway

The purpose of this article is to provide objective information on the technology available to those who require a significant amount of support in assisting their literacy development. Products are not compared critically because their relative merits will depend significantly on personal user needs. Those considering acquiring technology for this purpose are strongly advised to seek advice in selecting suitable equipment through the Government's Access to Work scheme or from an independent consultant.

There have been spectacular advances in voice recognition technology over the last twenty years, with DragonDictate® and Dragon NaturallySpeaking® (DNS) being the most successful products in that time. Although IBM ViaVoice is still available in PC stores, it is not recommended for those with a need for literacy support.

By far the most significant recent development has been the maturing of the Microsoft® voice recognition facility within the new Microsoft Vista operating system (Vista OS).

Many children who have difficulty articulating speech effectively or who have very strong regional or national accents and those with severe dyslexia need to dictate one word at a time to produce reasonably accurate text. This requires the use of a "discrete" voice recognition system such as DragonDictate. Despite the fact that software development ceased in 1997, purchasers of new equipment can legally retro-install Windows XP, giving DragonDictate an indefinite lease of life.

Those requiring literacy support when using a voice recognition system have two essential requirements, these being high recognition speed and accuracy and simplicity in its operation.

Table 1 compares various features of Vista VR with Dragon NaturallySpeaking, DragonDictate and IBM ViaVoice.

Feature	Product			
	Vista VR	DNS 10 Preferred®	DragonDictate® 60K ver 3.02	IBM ViaVoice® Pro 10
Cost (*)	Nil (microphone, say £30 per user)	£120 Per user	£150 per user	£150 per user
Mode of use	Continuous	Continuous	Discrete	Continuous
Accuracy unenrolled	90%	92%	85-90%	N/A
Accuracy enrolled	95-98%	95-98%	92-96%	92-98%
Typical (&) dictation speed	120 words per minute	120 words per minute	80 words per minute	110 words per minute
MS operating system	Vista	Vista or XP	XP or earlier	XP

*= excluding VAT; & =not including correction

Table 1: Comparison of features of voice recognition systems

The enrolment phase, during which the user speaks sample sentences before using the equipment, is now optional in Vista VR and DNS. The recognition system still adjusts to the user's voice as corrections are made; accuracy steadily increases thereafter. New words or phrases can be added to the vocabulary effortlessly as the system is used.

The Vista and DNS systems provide high levels of recognition performance from the outset for most users, i.e. good accuracy and high speed. However, this is not the limit of the demands made by those with literacy support needs.

Additional assistance through special support programs will be necessary to address one or more of the following:

- Checking for incorrect homophones in text (e.g. "rode" instead of "road). All recognition systems are capable of producing fairly frequent homophonic errors. Leaving such errors uncorrected can produce a chaotic effect in otherwise perfect text.

- Proof-reading document text. A text-to-speech (TTS) facility can be used to read out the text.

- Immediately confirming what has been dictated, through the echoing of the text which has been produced.

- Checking that spelling errors have not occurred through the voice recognition correction process. A good phonetically-based spell-checker is essential.

Over the years a number of support programs have been developed to address all these requirements in different ways. **KeyStone ScreenSpeaker** was the first to appear and was followed by **Read and Write** and then **ClaroRead**. Each of these provides the same general level of support for those generating text documents while also providing individual extras not found on the competitor products. They all provide:

- Homophone checking with the provision of alternatives

- Immediate echoing back (optionally) of text dictated by the user

- Sophisticated proof-reading by TTS of document text

- Advanced phonetically-based spell-checking of document text

Trainers working with people with literacy support needs have found that many users have difficulty in mastering voice recognition techniques. This frequently restricts their levels of achievement. **KeyStone SpeechTutor** was designed to address this problem and sets out to ensure that the early stages of using the technology are successful before moving to more advanced work.

Conclusion: The use of **Dragon NaturallySpeaking** or the **Microsoft Vista** voice recognition system provides an excellent tool to assist those with literacy support needs. Additional software is often essential to ensure success. Working with **KeyStone Speech Tutor** at the early stages and then moving towards **Read and Write, ClaroRead** or **KeyStone ScreenSpeaker** enables confidence to be maintained.

Function	Product			
	ClaroRead Plus 5.0	KeyStone Screen-Speaker	KeyStone SpeechTutor	Read & Write Gold
		10.0	3.2	9.0
Works with DNS?	•	•	•	•
Works with MS Vista voice?		•		
Works with DragonDictate?		• (version 7)		
Vary AVR echo characteristics?	•	•		
Works with internet?	•		•	
Works with MS Office?	•	Word only	Via clipboard	•
Works with general software?	•			•
TTS proof-reader?	•	•	•	•
Check for homophones?	•	•	(awaiting version 4)	•
Type of text-to-speech	RealSpeak	RealSpeak	Any SAPI-5 TTS	RealSpeak
Price (excluding VAT)	£160	£150	£95	£320

All products operate in Windows XP and Vista operating system and are regularly updated.

Table 2: Comparison of features of additional support software

Useful Web Sites

The following web sites provide further information on the systems described.

ClaroRead: http://www.clarosoftware.com/

Dragon NaturallySpeaking: www.nuance.com

KeyStone products and DragonDictate:
www.wordsworldwide.co.uk

Microsoft Vista VR: www.microsoft.com/enable/products/windowsvista/speech.aspx

Read & Write: http://www.texthelp.com/page.asp

Government Access to Work scheme:
http://www.direct.gov.uk/en/DisabledPeople/Employmentsupport/WorkSchemesAndProgrammes/DG_4000347

Note about the Author

Dr Peter Kelway is the Chairman of Words Worldwide Limited and has worked in the special needs arena for over twenty years. He has acted as a special needs assessor/ trainer and he designs software incorporating voice recognition and text-to-speech technology. You may contact him direct via:
psk@ www.wordsworldwide.co.uk.

4. Dyslexia Friendly Working Practices

4.1 Accessible Websites

Graeme Whippy

Introduction

The web has become an essential part of many people's lives, both at home and at work. Being denied access to information and services on the web can lead to social exclusion and can make it difficult to have a successful job or career.

In this section we explain what web accessibility is, why it is important and some pointers on things to consider when designing or building a website. We also provide some references for further information and reading.

What do we mean by 'web' and 'accessibility'?

The 'web' has moved far beyond its original purpose of enabling people to share information and documents; the technology behind the web now provides the means to deliver sophisticated functionality to users and the use of the web has spread from the public domain to companies where it is used to deliver information and systems.

So when we talk about the 'web' we include the following (with examples):

	Public	Private/Company
Information	News and entertainment sites Government sites Blogs, wikis and forums	Intranet Extranet
Services/Systems	Online banking Shopping	Expense submission Procurement

Accessibility can be defined as follows:

The usability of a product, service, environment or facility by people with the widest range of capabilities.

In the case of web accessibility it's about making websites (as defined above) usable by as many people as possible regardless of their capabilities, i.e. their ability to see, hear, use a mouse, read, etc.

Why bother about accessibility?

There are 4 very good reasons why companies should make their websites as accessible as possible:

Commercial

Denying people with disabilities access to your websites costs money; for a service provider it means there's a market segment you're not tapping into, for an employer it means that you're denying yourself access to the widest talent pool.

Being able to attract and retain disabled staff and customers is good for business and, like Corporate Responsibility, is no longer viewed as philanthropic or 'being nice'.

Technical

Accessible websites are well-built websites which bring a number of advantages, such as:

- Significantly smaller web pages (70% reduction is common) which reduces infrastructure demands, bandwidth utilization and download times.

- Increased text density on pages that improves search-ability and Search Engine rankings (e.g. Google).

- Reduced authoring and maintenance costs through increased simplicity of underlying code.

- Pages automatically display correctly when printed or displayed on alternative devices.

Usability

Accessible websites are easier for everyone to use, including those who do not have disabilities; this was demonstrated in research conducted by the Disability Rights Commission in 2004 which showed that people were able to complete tasks quicker on accessible websites than they were on less accessible websites.

This results in better service for customers and better productivity for staff, along with improved user experience, fewer errors, reduced training and fewer calls to the help desk.

Legal

The Disability Discrimination Act (DDA) makes it illegal to discriminate against people on the basis of their disabilities.

Dyslexia is a condition that is covered by the DDA and websites are cited in the DDA's code of practice. Therefore service providers and employers have a legal obligation to make their websites and web based systems accessible.

Pointers for Creating Accessible Websites

Creating accessible websites is really just about following best practice in website design and construction. It isn't about stripping back presentation, content and functionality to a lowest common denominator and it certainly isn't about making sites 'disabled friendly'. Such notions are outdated and not in keeping with modern, standards compliant web design.

In this section we provide some pointers to help you understand how to design and create websites that are generally accessible but with particular reference to dyslexia.

Structure and Navigation

The foundation for a successful, easy to use and accessible website is clear structure (how the site and its pages are organized) and navigation (how to move around the site).

At any time the visitor to the site must be able to know where they are, where they can go and where they have been.

There are various techniques you can use to help make structure and navigation clear. For example:

- Define page regions that follow a standard convention and are consistently placed on every page, e.g. main menu, left menu, footer links, utility links, main content, supplementary content.

- Maintain navigational 'context', e.g. highlight the currently selected menu items, provide a 'crumbtrail' to the current page.

- Differentiate visited links from unvisited links, e.g. use a slightly different colour.

- Be wary of using icons for menu items unless the icons are very obvious; forcing the user to roll the mouse over an icon in order to understand what it does will reduce usability.

- Have a clear link back to the home page on every page.

- As a rule of thumb it is recommended that a 7 ± 2 rule be used for the number of items at a given level in a menu, this being a comfortable number for people to digest and remember, particularly important for people with dyslexia who may struggle in this respect.

- Sitemaps are not essential if the site has an intuitive structure and a reliable and convenient search facility is provided.

Content

Structure provides a framework for a website's content, the words and pictures that give people a reason to visit or use your site.

It's important to remember that people read on-line differently to the way they read from paper and adjust your writing style accordingly.

The following pointers can help ensure that your content is as accessible as possible:

- Use the simplest language possible (taking into account the likely needs and reading ability of the target users).

- Have one main theme/message per page.

- Use 'inverse pyramid' style of writing where the conclusion/ main point comes first followed by more detail.

- Keep paragraphs short and to the point, e.g. the BBC News site uses one sentence per paragraph.

- Always expand abbreviations and acronyms the first time they are used on every page.

- Provide alternative forms of content where you think people might benefit, e.g. pictures to support words or words to support pictures.

- Provide a description for every image using its 'Alt' text for the benefit of visually impaired users. If the image does not warrant a description then use empty Alt text ("").

- Make sure that captions and transcripts are provided for video or audio content so that people unable to hear/see are still able to access the content.

Presentation

Presentation is used to make web pages look attractive, engaging, more usable and improve the overall user experience so that not only do people benefit from visiting/using the site but find it pleasurable and rewarding.

The following pointers will help ensure that the presentation used is accessible in particular to people with dyslexia.

- Do not use a pure white background to pages; people with dyslexia often find that white backgrounds - especially on screen - make reading far more difficult. It is better to use a pastel shade like cream (see the bullet on preferences below).

- Make sure that foreground and background colours have sufficient contrast. Failing to do so will make the content hard to read, especially for older people and those with visual impairment.

- Do not use serif fonts like Times Roman as these are harder to read than sans-serif fonts like Arial.

- Only use italics to *emphasise* particular words, not for cosmetic effect. Italicised text is harder to read than non-italicised.

- Do not underline text as people may confuse this with links.

- Left align text, do not fully justify it and be wary of centring it; left aligned text is much easier to read for everybody, especially people with dyslexia.

- Leave plenty of whitespace in and around text, for example between paragraphs and between regions on the page. Cramming as much content as possible into a page can be very hard to read and understand.

- Use headings to break up and group text in a page: think of the headings being a table of contents of the page that helps people gain a quick understanding of what the page contains.

- Avoid using text images, e.g. fancy headings, because the size and colour of text in images cannot be changed by the user (see next point).

- Enable people to make changes to presentation according to their own preferences, e.g. changing foreground/background colours or the font size. (Note that although this can be done using built-in browser features not everybody knows that such features exist and they are not always easy to find and use).

- Consider providing text-to-speech tools on the website. Alternatively provide information on software that can be used on all websites and documents.

Functionality

Functionality is the features provided in a website that go beyond static information. This can be something simple like a 'concertina' effect where content is shown/hidden when the user clicks on a link, or a full blown application like on-line banking or a company expense system.

There are 3 essential guidelines when it comes to accessible functionality:

- Make sure that functionality can be used without the mouse because not everybody is able to use one (e.g. blind people, people with RSI). It's therefore essential that functionality can be used with just the keyboard.

- Always provide the means to go 'back' in a process; for example, if you are presenting a multi-page form always enable the person to go back to a previous page in the form. This enables users to go back and make changes or correct mistakes rather than having to start from scratch or give up.

- JavaScript can greatly improve usability but it must be used in an accessible way. For example, you must ensure that it can be invoked with the keyboard and that the user is made aware of and can access the results of the JavaScript. You should also make sure that there is an acceptable fall-back in case the user does not have JavaScript enabled.

Best Practice

Lastly there are some things that should be done when building a website that impact accessibility and are general best practice:

- Use HTML tags correctly. For example, when you add headings to a page use the HTML H1, H2, H3 etc tags and don't just make text big and bold. Likewise, don't use the heading tags just to make text look big and bold. The same principle applies to lists (don't create pseudo lists), block quotes (don't use these for indenting text) and tables (these should be only used for presenting tabular information).

- Make sure that the HTML is valid. Not all browsers are tolerant of incorrect HTML so one of the best ways to make sure your web pages look and work correctly in Internet Explorer, Firefox, Safari, Chrome etc. is to ensure that the HTML is written in accordance with World Wide Web Consortium (W3C) standards and contains no errors.

- Use Cascading Style Sheets (CSS) to control presentation and layout rather than embedding it into the HTML of the page using tags, attributes and tables. This has a number of disadvantages including preventing people from viewing the page in accordance with their own preferences.

Further Information

The following are recommended as sources of further information:

WCAG 2.0

The Worldwide Web Consortium's (W3C) Web Content Accessibility Guidelines. Quoting the W3C: "Following these guidelines will make content accessible to a wider range of people with disabilities, including blindness and low vision, deafness and hearing loss, learning disabilities, cognitive limitations, limited movement, speech disabilities, photosensitivity and combinations of these."

There is a wealth of information available on WCAG 2 at the W3C's site: www.w3.org/TR/WCAG20.

PAS 78

Publicly Available Specification (PAS) 78 is a guide to best practice in commissioning accessible websites. It is aimed at 'commissioners', i.e. the people paying an agency or consultancy to create a website.

PAS 78 is available for download from the Equality and Human Rights Commission's website:

http://www.equalityhumanrights.com/en/publicationsandresources/Pages/PAS78.aspx.

BS 8878

BS 8878 is the formalising of PAS 78 into a British Standard in best practice in commissioning accessible websites. It was released as a Draft for Public Comment in December 2008 and is expected to be published in April 2009.

BS 8878 is available for review at www.drafts.bsigroup.com.

DRC 2004 Formal Investigation into Web Accessibility

In 2004 the Disability Rights Commission (DRC) undertook research on web accessibility in the UK. The findings included the fact that 80% of sites did not meet a basic level of accessibility as stipulated by the W3C. The report and its findings are essential reading for people interested in web accessibility and the issues faced by disabled people. The report resulted the creation of PAS 78 and BS 8878.

The report can be downloaded from the Equality and Human Rights Commission's website:

www.equalityhumanrights.com/en/publicationsandresources/Pages/webaccess.aspx.

4.2 Shared Responsibility

Judi Stewart, Chief Executive, British Dyslexia
Association

Adulthood brings independence and responsibility, which in
many ways is welcome. Independence sounds a little more
interesting than responsibility but the two go hand in hand.
Independence is only acceptable to others if it is within the
norms of the society in which we live. Individuals need to
take responsibility for their actions, and societal and legal
frameworks set the limits on what will be tolerated.

What happens if people are not equal, which is the case when
we are talking about adults who are dyslexic? Should there
be special treatment and if so what should that treatment be?
These are big questions that are not easy to answer as no two
dyslexic adults have the same strengths and weaknesses and
therefore 'blanket' solutions can only be part of the answer.

Let's look at what 'blanket' solutions are provided in the UK.
The key 'blanket' solution is an Act within the legal framework
- the Disability Discrimination Act (2005). Dyslexia is defined
as a disability and as such an employer must make reasonable
adjustments to reduce the impact the disability has on an
employee's ability to perform in their job. Immediately, and
quite rightly, the employer is brought into the equation. There
is also support for the dyslexic adult and the employer through
Government schemes such as Access to Work, which is a
scheme run by Jobcentre Plus. Here the dyslexic adult who is
either in a paid job, unemployed and about to start a job or
self employed can apply for the cost of reasonable adjustments,
for example, equipment or a support worker to be paid in part

or in full. Jobcentre Plus also helps find work for unemployed people, particularly long-term unemployed or people with disabilities.

If we take the law as the framework on which all this sits so far we have two stakeholders, the Government and the employer.

The missing stakeholder is the dyslexic adult. All three stakeholders hold some power and all three must take responsibility.

The Government and the employer need to work together to create a platform where the dyslexic adult can thrive and the dyslexic adult needs to engage in the opportunities presented. However, many dyslexic adults and employers do not know that help, such as Access to Work, is available and others do not manage to work the system even though they have become aware of it. The British Dyslexia Association receives literally hundreds of calls to its national Helpline from frustrated dyslexic job seekers or those in work who are afraid of losing their job. Here we have a case of a 'blanket' solution that offers hope but it does not go quite far enough. Awareness and delivery need to be an even greater part of the package.

A 'blanket' solution is the first step but, by their very nature they have to be interpreted to apply to an individual situation. There are many occasions where the 'blanket' solutions do not solve the problem and the only way to resolve an issue long term is a balance between the 'blanket' solutions and the people who act out those solutions. Laws and rules can only go so far and they will never cover every eventuality. It is people who will make the real changes. In other words as well as the law there needs to be a cultural change that leads to a change in behaviour, attitudes and values.

Access to Work is a good example of how an agency has listened and adapted. At the end of 2008 Access to Work removed the need for a dyslexic adult to prove they are dyslexic. Up until this point dyslexia was the only disability where the individual had to prove their disability. This welcome news has certainly not resolved all the issues around getting the right support for dyslexic people at work but it is a step in the right direction.

For dyslexic adults, trying to enter employment can be very difficult especially if they have no history of employment or other qualifications. Here it is up to the Government to make sure that there are suitable opportunities and support to enable the dyslexic adult to move to a position where they can take responsibility and be independent adults. The British Dyslexia Association is campaigning for more relevant opportunities because at present many of the options only provide the same type of teaching that led to failure at school.

Every employer should want to support a dyslexic employee to realise their value and potential, not feel compelled to make reasonable adjustments because it is the law. This change of attitude immediately breaks down the barriers. No one is suggesting that a dyslexic person should be employed to do a job just because they are dyslexic. They are either applying for a job because they believe they have the necessary skills or they are in employment because at one point they demonstrated that they had the necessary skills and experience.

Barriers exist within a job, some as a direct effect of the employer and some through outside agencies such as those who set professional exams which need to be passed to open up further career opportunities. Here the number of stakeholders begins to increase but it is the responsibility of the three key stakeholders to do something about it - the Government, the employer and the dyslexic adult.

Problems often occur as an employee is promoted or moved to another job within an organisation. The employee either used coping strategies or their dyslexia was not a problem in the original job. The new role may require other skills that move the dyslexic adult out of their comfort zone. The dyslexic adult needs to be able to understand their dyslexia and what coping strategies might be relevant or to ask for professional advice without fear of recrimination. The wise employer will listen and act, knowing that in most cases a reasonably simple solution can be found. In rare cases this new role may not be suitable for this particular employee but it is only through openness, understanding and each party taking responsibility that a sensible solution can be found.

Many dyslexic adults hide their dyslexia because of fear. Fear that they will be laughed at, not taken seriously or overlooked when it comes to promotion. This fear is often learnt behaviour that comes from being teased at school or in the workplace. There is also little understanding in the workplace of what dyslexia is and how to support a dyslexic person. Comments and the attitude of colleagues are just as important as the way management acts. Staff tend to follow the example of senior managers and senior managers need to lead by example. All staff need general awareness of dyslexia and then they can treat their dyslexic colleague appropriately and without fuss.

To be a truly dyslexic-friendly society responsibility needs to be shared between the Government, the employer and the dyslexic adult. 'Blanket' solutions provide a framework and then it is up to those representing the Government and the employer to bring down the barriers and provide the opportunities. The dyslexic adult must play their part and take advantage of those opportunities. Very often this means extra work for the dyslexic adult but no one can learn for another human being, all they can do is provide the opportunity.

The rest is up to the individual concerned.

4.3 Case Study

Mike Poole, Personal Trainer

"I've been in sales since I was 17 years old but it wasn't a lifelong ambition of mine. It was a tough decision to leave work and study at home for a new career, especially when my dyslexia restricts me from following some career paths.

However, I have no regrets as my passion has always been for sport. When I was younger, I competed on a national level as a water polo goalkeeper so I knew working in the fitness industry was something I'd enjoy."

Mike embarked on a Personal Training Diploma in 2007 with Lifetime Health and Fitness: "Being dyslexic, it is very important for me that learning isn't all about reading and writing. My course offered the variety I needed, the tutors were amazing and it was the personal touch that helped me stay motivated.

"I loved every bit of the diploma. It was great to take my previous knowledge further and explore why we have to do certain exercises and eat certain things. The course was challenging but I've never used my dyslexia as an excuse - it just spurred me on even further to gain the qualification."

Mike has since radically changed his career direction from Sales Manager to personal trainer.

He adds: "I've managed to put the passion back into my work-life. My job is so diverse that I never get bored. There's nothing better than seeing a client recover from a long term injury. Plus, I can continue playing and coaching water polo so my job is more like a hobby.

"My advice for those who have dyslexia would be to take your time and look for a course that can provide you with the learning support you need. It's important to remember that having dyslexia or another SpLD doesn't have to be a barrier to reaching your goals."

4.4 Creativity - Harnessing Talent

Kevin Morley, Vice President, British Dyslexia Association

Standing in front of Professor Congdon with my son, then aged 6, made me realise that this dyslexia thing had a lot of different sides to it.

Let me go back 19 years to when Stephen was diagnosed by Professor Congdon and he confirmed our suspicions that he was dyslexic, but it was what he said about dyslexia that has stayed with me for the ensuing 19 years. He told me that Stephen would on occasion be distracted, go into a daydream, and that we should under no circumstances disturb this daydream. "It is during one of these moments," he said, "that he could invent a cure for cancer."

It made me realise that dyslexia is largely about creativity and that dyslexics, although "wired up differently" tend to be extremely creative.

Fast forward a dozen years, and I have the opportunity to put this theory to the staunchest commercial test, as I find myself running one of the fastest growing advertising agencies in the country, and yes, it has a creative department. The two best creatives I had at the time were both dyslexic. They were both a little mad too, but I guess you can put that down to their "creative tension." Alas, in this country as opposed to say America, creatives take themselves very seriously indeed.

Now it's true that I didn't go out specifically to find and then recruit dyslexics for the creative department. There was no element of "positive discrimination", but by the same token, I was never inclined to reject any candidate because of his or her dyslexia, the opposite is true.

Indeed, such was the success of the existing crop of dyslexic creatives, I was far more inclined to recruit more dyslexics than other less "gifted" individuals.

The fact that I had just been asked to be a Vice President of the BDA helped a little as well, I suppose!

So having established that there is a link between dyslexia and creativity how important is creativity in the world now and in the future? Let me quote Charles Handy, the eminent business thinker and writer and formerly a Professor at London Business School:

"The coming of the information economy offers the tantalising promise of a modern alchemy, the ability to create wealth out of nothing. Microsoft stands as a sort of parable of our times, for it was built on nothing but the ideas and energies of two people.

The modern economies will not be constrained by lack of resources but only by lack of creativity and ideas."

Similarly, when I was asked to give the Keynote Speech to the World Marketing Forum in Cologne a few gears ago, my theme was creativity. Without creative minds in a creative environment, the West is commercially doomed. If all manufacturing is carried out by low paid workers in low cost countries, where does that leave us? We in the West have to be the ideas people, the creatives who constantly invent new orders and original processes.

Harvard Business School actually has a course in creativity, given by John Kao. He believes, together with the Nomura Institute, the world's economic activity can be divided into three distinct areas:

we have gone from Agriculture to Industry to Information. Right now, be believes, we are entering the fourth era: the Creative Age.

In a recent interview he said;

> *"The search for value has led companies to seek efficiency through downsizing, rationalising and right-sizing: approaches that eventually result in a diminishing level of return. But what will fuel growth in the future? Growth will come through mastering the skills of creativity; and making creativity actionable."*

So these are the views of two thoughtful and perceptive people, who believe fervently that creativity is the key to future success, both individually and collectively.

This puts dyslexic people in pole position for a successful future world if they can only recognise their innate creativity and harness it.

And therein lies the rub. Can they harness it? There is always a downside, and it is this.

Although around 10% of the population of Great Britain has some elements of dyslexia (and I know that estimates vary, but this one will do for now), 30 - 50% of the prison population is estimated to be dyslexic. Yes, up to half of all prisoners currently serving time may be dyslexic, a shocking figure.

So how does that happen? My theory is that, with creativity comes emotional baggage which is not always a positive force. I remember clearly when certain creatives in the advertising agency had their ideas rejected, they became frustrated and angry. Now if this frustration takes hold, in certain people it could lead to violence, and maybe that is the reason for such a high proportion of prisoners being dyslexic, but frankly nobody knows. It could be something as simple as creativity being misdirected towards less than totally legal activities, but it certainly says to me that more research in this area would be helpful.

The key to everything in the world of dyslexia is early recognition. I was extremely fortunate with my son, because of my connections with the BDA. It quickly became apparent that he was brilliant at numbers but less so at words, and in particular spelling. He also had a habit of going off into a world of his own, and it was this aspect of his behaviour that Professor Congdon honed in on. This was nearly 20 years ago, when dyslexia officially didn't exist. Schools resisted the temptation to recognise dyslexia as it would mean that they would then have to allocate resources to look after the needs of dyslexics, and it is largely thanks to the work done by the BDA that dyslexia is recognised by the Education Department today.

Only by early recognition of dyslexia by parents and schools will this innate creativity be harnessed and the frustration coming out of confusion will be eradicated. In fact, schools have a duty to recognise dyslexia, and nurture those children who are dyslexic, because in the world described by both Charles Handy and John Kao, the future will belong to the creative elements of our society. Only creatives will prosper, they argue, so the creative dyslexic is to be cherished for there lies all our futures.

So how did my dyslexic son fare in the creative world? Well gaining the Design Prize at Eton for 5 years in a row, followed by a Masters Degree in Engineering at Cambridge - that tells its own story!

4.5 Coping Strategies

Lord Addington, Vice President, British Dyslexia Association

My coping strategies for dealing with dyslexia are both possible and encouraged by the simple fact that I'm a member of Parliament. What this means is that in my environment I am a valued, indeed cherished part of the establishment and the establishment thus has a vested interest in making my life at least tolerable. That combined with the fact that parliament is something worthy, use of the spoken word is the primary objective of us being there (even in a world obsessed by getting press attention and compiling blogs the spoken word is the most important part of the job) this gives me an advantage that very few dyslexic people have.

Just to give an example: I don't use notes when I speak which means I have the advantage of not having to combine looking down at the piece of paper with trying to at least give the impression that I am interested in the people I am talking to, (to anyone who's ever had to sit through a speech where all you can see is the top of the person's head as they deliver it you will get the idea), and this also helps with voice projection. Very well known politicians are to this day astounded by the fact that I can deliver a 10 minute speech without having notes. The simple fact is as a dyslexic MP I do not regard a piece of paper with writing on it as a safety blanket but rather a trip hazard.

However the maintenance of the office, by that I mean the normal correspondence and chasing around the information, does present many more problems.

My primary way of compensating for not being able to easily knock out letters, or increasingly e-mails, has always been to get hold of a telephone number and to speak to the people. It should be noted that any member of the House of Lords who phones people, particularly if it's about work in the House of Lords, is probably in a pretty strong position to, for instance, get a verbal briefing about a subject. I am very well aware that most dyslexic people do not enjoy this privileged position particularly when dealing with forms etc.

The other great standby is that old favourite, smiling at people, telling them you are dyslexic and asking for help. I have also found that telling somebody that you can't do something or you can't do it quickly, gets a much better response than saying you have a little bit of a problem with something. It's a bit like someone who is going down a motorway who sees somebody broken down on the hard shoulder and will probably feel some sympathy for them, whereas somebody who is stuck in third gear in front of you is simply a bloody nuisance. I would not say that I always find it easy to ask for help but the fact of the matter is that it means things get done that otherwise wouldn't.

Over the past few years I have become a more consistent user of voice operated technology with my computer (as the technology has improved it has become much easier. I did actually keep one piece of writing initially produced by the very early Dragon Systems which had all the mistakes caused by simply breathing on the less advanced microphones, combinations of words which I feel had never been used before or since!). The use of voice operated computing is making normal office communication much easier but even this requires something of a cultural shift particularly among work colleagues: it tends to curtail office chat and until your colleagues know about it you occasionally get rather strange looks as you speak in a rather staccato fashion to a computer screen.

I'm currently familiarising myself with Dragon 10 which does seem to be a considerable improvement on what went before. Maybe next year I will be able to give you a more definitive answer.

To summarise, the basic thrust of all my coping strategies is to let people know what they're dealing with, try and tell them as clearly as I can what I can and can't do, particularly in certain circumstances and under pressure of time, and to try and remember to say thank you when they try to help. For those who are unhelpful, well I usually have the whip hand over them as it is normally to do with parliament, and the odd tactful reminder of the Disability Discrimination Act has on occasions worked wonders.

Lord Addington is the Liberal Democrat Deputy Chief Whip in the House of Lords.

Having dyslexia has encouraged him to lend his support to the British Dyslexia Association and take the position of Vice-President. He is also Vice-President of the UK Sports Association.

4.6 Designing Dyslexia Friendly Reading Materials

Patience Thomson

Introduction

The most important thing to think about when you are writing for dyslexics is KISS - Keep It Short and Simple. This can be hard work. The French philosopher Pascal once said that he had written a long letter because he had no time to write a short one.

To get your point across you have to plan with care what you want to say and how you want to say it. The important question will be not only, "Did I say everything I wanted to say?" but also "Has the other person taken it all in?".

Teachers at school say they have taught all their lesson plans for the term, but how much of it do the pupils remember? "It's all there in the instructions," someone tells you as you struggle to put up a tent for the family holiday. But the instructions may be gobble-de-gook to you. You are sitting in the car. "This is how you get there," says your friend, explaining in detail all the twists and turns and the BP garage on your right. You drive round the corner and you have forgotten the lot.

Dyslexic people often need rather more time to take in and digest words, just as many of them like to be given extra time to find the right words to express themselves. They can easily drown in words if the volume is too great. If you are a less confident cyclist you need a smooth road. If you are a less confident reader, you need the language of what you read to be crystal clear. Moreover, you want it presented in a form where the information you are looking for can be easily found. Otherwise, the effort you have to spend trying to work out the sounds of the words robs you of the chance to keep up with the meaning of the text.

10 years ago I co-founded a Publishing Company, Barrington Stoke, to produce attractive materials for the reluctant reader. Our customers were of all ages and all were hesitant readers. We asked them to tell us what they felt about every aspect of the books. My big fear was that each individual would have different problems and we couldn't solve them all. It didn't work out that way. They agreed with each other almost all the time.

First, we needed to find out how they would like the text arranged and presented on the page to make it easier to grasp. Then we looked at the content. We found out from them all the factors that made a text hard or easy to read, and understand.

Rather than telling you what I think you should do to create dyslexia friendly reading materials, I am going to tell you very simply what the dyslexic readers would like you to do.

Presentation

The way that material is presented can help or hinder readers who have difficulties with either visual perception or visual memory.

- Quite a few dyslexics are sensitive to the kind of bright lights you find in a classroom or office. Printing on off-white or even cream paper softens the harsh effect of black on white. It is easier for some dyslexic people to write on coloured paper too.

- The paper must be of good quality so that the print from the other side does not show through.

- The print should not be too small and dense, but it should also not be too large. This is because, if we are going to read well, we must take in whole groups of words at a time. If the words are too large we cannot focus enough in one go. Point 13 is about right.

- For the same reason the columns of print should not be too narrow. This can be a problem with newspapers or bulletins.

- Having slightly wider spaces between letters, words and lines makes an amazing difference. An r and an n too close together, for instance, look very like an m.

- The type-face should be a familiar one such as Times New Roman. Dyslexic readers react to small differences, perhaps because they read more slowly and intensely.

- Words should not be split between two lines.

- If there are illustrations or photographs it should be clear which lines of print they refer to. They should not stray over the text.

- Text is much harder to read if the right hand margin is justified. Dyslexic readers do not like adjusted spacing between the words. A more ragged margin on the right makes it much easier for them to keep their place.

- Flow diagrams are easier to understand and remember than linear notes that go down the page from top to bottom.

- Charts and graphs are easier than rows of figures.

- It is good to divide up the text. The creative use of headings and subheadings, shadowed text, bold type and italics are all very helpful. One small point should be remembered. Capital letters are not helpful. Words look too uniform and have no shape, compare IMPORTANT with important.

All these points may seem quite small on their own but taken together they make a huge difference.

Content and Language

It has long been assumed that the length of words and sentences are the most important factor in determining the level of reading difficulty of a particular text. Of course this does matter but it is only part of the story.

Skill is needed to simplify the text without making it sound childish or patronising.

- The first couple of paragraphs of any text are the most important. Too many hard words from the start will make the reader lose confidence.

- The words need to be familiar. This matters more than their length. Use simpler words whenever you can - " at once" rather than "immediately".

- If hard words must be included, make sure they are well spaced out "Significantly increased expenditure" would make dyslexic readers stop and struggle and they would lose their thread.

- Paragraphs should not be too long and each should have a specific point. To check on this ask yourself, "What question does this paragraph answer for me?"

- Sentences do not all have to be short, indeed it will spoil the rhythm and flow if they are. Use simple conjunctions like "and" and "but" to join up the different parts.

- Do not invert the sentence so the main point gets lost. "' watched TV instead of doing his homework," is easier "Instead of doing his homework he watched TV".

- The paragraphs should run in an orderly sequence. To test if this is happening try converting them into a flow diagram. Do they all stick to the point?

- Concrete words that can easily be linked to an image in the mind (aeroplane, calculator) are easier to read than abstract words, especially adverbs, that have no precise meaning. Is "hardly" the opposite of "softly?"

- The active tense is much easier than the passive - "he had a good idea", rather than "he was struck by a good idea ".

- Gerunds and gerundives are confusing - "On the way back he saw" is preferred to "coming back he saw".

- Beware of acronyms, e.g. CIA, which may be unfamiliar to the inexperienced reader.

Any or all of these ideas will help dyslexics. They have been well tested in the field and it is worth trying them out.

5. Supporting Dyslexic Individuals

5.1 Dyslexia and Unemployment

Alan Shoreman

Traditionally dyslexia and its related problems have been seen as purely based in the learning spectrum, particularly relating to children and post-compulsory education. Unfortunately, the reality is quite different and, as we are aware, most people with dyslexia go through life unrecognised and in many cases unaware of their disability. Employment, or more to the point unemployment, is an area that is greatly under- researched and there is little in the way of robust and large-scale investigation into a possible correlation of dyslexia and benefit dependency.

There were two small studies carried out in the North West in recent years. Helen Boden, working for The British Dyslexia Association assessed 50 unemployed customers who had been identified as having literacy issues, from four Jobcentres in and around Manchester. Of the 50 customers, 48 of them could be classed as having a high percentage of dyslexia. In 2001, Dyslexia Access, working in Sefton, Merseyside suggested 40 per cent of Job Seekers Allowance recipients were positively for dyslexia traits. From these two small studies could be assumed that there is a high probability who have dyslexia are disproportionately represented in Department for Work and Pensions unemployment

The Disability Discrimination Act 2005 defines disability as "a physical or mental impairment that has a substantial and long term adverse effect on his or her ability to carry out normal day-to-day activities." Dyslexia is a disability; it impacts on a person throughout their lives, in education, in work and in accessing goods and services. Due to the nature of dyslexia it is considered by many to be a hidden disability, as it is not always apparent to the untrained eye, and identification can be difficult. Many people leaving compulsory education without meaningful qualifications are at a considerable disadvantage when trying to gain employment.

There has been a substantial change in Britain over the past 25 years in the types of jobs that were common to our country.

Post-War Britain saw the creation of the Welfare State and huge investment in construction and manufacturing that generated blue collared jobs and in-work training. In these times, work for those without qualifications or with poor literacy was not as hard to come by as it is today. There has been a massive change in the employment market over the last quarter of the 20th Century and beyond. With the development of more service and administrative industries such as banking, insurance, customer-focused and clerical work, minimum levels of numeracy and literacy are essential. This was highlighted in ⸱e Government's Welfare to Work Report, which included Lord ⸱h's findings:

⸱rity for all in the Global Economy:
⸱lass Skills

⸱ord Leitch found that:

⸱ent of those with no qualifications are out bal economy changes, the employment opportunities of those lacking a platform of skills will fall still further. The millions of adults lacking functional literacy and numeracy skills risk becoming a lost generation, increasingly cut off from labour market opportunity. Equipping disadvantaged groups with a platform of skills will be increasingly essential to improving their employment."

Many may argue that the key to gaining and sustaining employment is due more to the acquirements of skills rather than qualifications. As it stands at the moment, almost all academic and vocational qualifications require a high level of literacy and numeracy. A high proportion of adults with dyslexia are seriously disadvantaged due to their reading and writing difficulties and will not reproduce their understanding or knowledge of a subject in the written word. This in itself marginalizes many individuals who may have the potential and skills to excel in the workplace.

Identification is a barrier that many people with dyslexia fail to clear as they struggle through life without recognition or support.

Major contributions to this are manifold and include lack of awareness, lack of resources and the cost of dyslexia assessments. In education, schools, colleges and universities, formal recognition is required to access support, which usually consists of a clinical or educational psychologist assessment. These assessments can be extremely expensive and will run in hundreds of pounds. Therefore, for most people on benefits low incomes the option of a full assessment is highly unlik However, for many of those who may be seeking emplo or are struggling in the workplace, a full assessment n not always be required. Given some of the excellent screening tools now available, interventions and rr be swift and cost effective.

Remploy is a non-Departmental Government-funded organisation and the biggest employer of disabled people in Britain. Last year Remploy also supported over six thousand disabled people into mainstream employment. The company's Specialist Services Department has now been running a dyslexia project for over two years. They have thirty employment advisers who are trained and accredited to BTEC level three in Dyslexia Awareness, Recognition and Analysis, which was provided by Adult Dyslexia Access based in Liverpool. Initially, the project was piloted in the North West and was used only to identify those who indicate having high levels of significant traits of dyslexia. The project has developed substantially in the past two years, developing the tool to map dyslexia traits against suitable vocational areas, and this has the potential to support great numbers of people into sustainable employment.

Although still in its early days, Remploy is now seeing the beneficial outcomes of the project. The screenings have been seen to not only identify candidates showing dyslexia traits but also accurately provide vocational indicators. The Dyslexia Vocational Evaluation comprises of three main elements. Firstly, there is a semi-structured qualitative interview, which looks at family history, schooling, day-to-day activities and employment. The standard Vinegrad questionnaire of 20 closed questions is then used to add additional support to the evaluation. Then, a computerised psychometric screening tool is used to measure a number of issues and strengths that characterise dyslexia. We have found that all candidates screened, who have subsequently been through a full assessment, have without exception been identified as having dyslexia. Finally a structured report has been designed to take the strengths identified and map them to appropriate vocational areas.

Remploy also offers support to people with dyslexia in work and whose job may be at risk due to their disability. Retention in the workplace is a big part of Remploy's services, offering advice and guidance to a wide range of people in many diverse occupations.

In recent times Remploy has successfully supported many people with dyslexia including a NHS clinical psychologist, police officers, civil servants, factory workers and supermarket staff. Remploy has drawn on over sixty years of experience of supporting disabled people in employment and can now transfer its knowledge and expertise into identifying people with dyslexia and helping them to overcome employment barriers.

Evidence would suggest that people with dyslexia are far more likely to be unemployed or at risk of losing their jobs than those without traits of dyslexia. However, given the correct recognition, support and interventions, they can become highly valued and productive employees. It is well known that a great number of people with dyslexia possess flare and ingenuity that has transformed the world of industry.

5.2 Case Study
Ki McRoberts, Singer/Songwriter

I was diagnosed with severe dyslexia at eight years old. My primary school up until that point refused to believe I had dyslexia, and I received very little support from them. While at school I also experienced bullying for many years due to not being able to read or write, which affected me greatly.

I left primary school not able to even spell my own name properly, and with very little self-confidence.

Once in secondary school things did improve. I was able to get a specialist tutor to teach me how to read and write, but after three years the extra support stopped. The knock on effect of this led me to truant from school, and only passing one GCSE in art.

I did however stay on an extra year at school, and then went onto Art College, and later Brighton Art School. During my time in Higher Education I found writing essays very difficult. There was no real help for people with dyslexia at the time, and due to being heavily criticised by a tutor at Brighton Art School for my problems with dyslexia, I decided to leave the education system all together.

The only real downside for me not having many qualifications has been facing the grim task of low paid work and, at times, unemployment. It can be really hard, and I think people experiencing problems with dyslexia who are unemployed must find it difficult, as there doesn't seem to be much support for them.

Fortunately, my interest in art, photography and music helped me a lot, and has led me to become a singer/songwriter. Also my experiences with dyslexia inspired me to set up Resolution Daes, which is a music based project to help raise further awareness and support for people with dyslexia. I am currently organising my projects' first UK tour, which I will also be headlining.

I believe that everything happens for a reason, and that no matter what you're labelled with or how tough life can be, as long as you truly believe in yourself you can turn your dreams into a reality.

5.3 Working with Dyslexia in the Healthcare and Emergency Services

Carol Leather, Independent Dyslexia Consultants, British Dyslexia Association Organisational Member.

People are often surprised to discover that many dyslexic people work in the Healthcare and Emergency services, but there are very good reasons why this should be so. These professions involve utilizing skills which are commonly recognised as dyslexic strengths: practical skills - those who can quickly construct a ladder system to get to an almost inaccessible window; good problem solving and strategic planning skills - the paramedic who can take control and calm things down in life threatening situations; good people skills - the nurse who can easily persuade the sick but stubborn child to take his medicine.

The demands of some public service roles are very different from those of office-based work. There can be a risk critical and public safety element to the job role. The role may require a rapid assessment of circumstances, clear and accurate communication at speed, great accuracy when recording information and the ability to react quickly to changing environments, as well as being able to produce reports or written documentation quickly. Some jobs may require considerable multitasking, for example giving a commentary or detailed information over the radio while driving at speed in an unfamiliar area. For some dyslexic people producing the written work will be the only problem for them as they thrive in rapidly changing circumstances, while for others learning to do the multitasking aspects of the job at an automatic level may take them longer. Dyslexic people should be given the opportunity to develop their skills to a competent level. However, in these risk critical occupations it is important that the competencies required to do the job are achieved so that the integrity of the job and also of dyslexic people is not compromised.

Under the DDA organisations are required to make reasonable adjustments for dyslexic people; these adjustments are to 'level the playing field'. Dyslexia affects everyone differently, therefore these adjustments must be specific to the individual, evidence based and relevant to the job. Often general recommendations are put into place for specific difficulties and this can be counterproductive. Recommendations for reasonable adjustments are best made by people who have a very good understanding of dyslexia, the impact it can have on an individual and the particular job role.

Before some adjustments can be put into place the individual must be prepared to disclose their dyslexia. Research suggests that many people do not disclose as they do not know what to say and they fear that they will be misunderstood. Owing to the diversity of dyslexia, being able to advocate for what one needs to work well is essential. They need to be able to outline their difficulties and some solutions should be explored with their managers. These may include:

- some extra time to learn new procedures,
- extra training,
- to clarify information several times without being misunderstood,
- to ask for reminders,
- to receive briefing notes in advance of meetings,

- not to be a minute taker at the case conference,

- not to have to read aloud,

- to be given an overview of key points in a report before reading it.

It is important to recognise that the impact of dyslexia is contextual. In times of transition, promotion or changes to the role particular problems may arise, but with a little extra input these can often be easily dealt with. Often general assumptions are made about people with very specific difficulties e.g. the very competent police officer who was penalised for struggling to record number plates accurately. This matter became a much bigger issue than it should have done as her manager assumed that as she couldn't do this apparently simple task and she was dyslexic she must be incompetent. In reality two sessions of specialist coaching enabled her to develop strategies to solve the problem. Now she continues to be a successful police officer.

Dyslexic People should not forget to say what they can do well!

In order to disclose, it is important that the employers provide an environment in which people feel comfortable to do so. Dyslexic people need to be sure their employers will see them first as people with skills rather than just dyslexic.

Disability policies and easy access to information about dyslexia, and the provision of services and support systems, and awareness training for managers and trainers all contribute to this.

An Organisational Case Study

In anticipation of the DDA, in 2003 a police service sought advice from dyslexia specialists. This led to a strategic approach:

- awareness training days throughout the whole organisation, particularly for management,

- specialist training for the police trainers,

- assessment of and one-to-one tuition for trainee police officers.

Initially, the first and third aspects were adopted. Awareness training days were run and the students at the training college had access to assessment and specialist one-to-one skills training. Within three years it was decided to train the police trainers to screen for dyslexia and provide specialist support. This was done for two reasons: it was more cost-effective as so many students were benefiting from the provision; but, more importantly, because the police trainers had a better understanding of the job and what was being asked of the students, they were therefore able to give more targeted and appropriate support. All the learning support team now have dyslexia specialist training. They screen students using the Dyslexia Adult Screening Test and make recommendations about reasonable adjustments such as allowing extra time to complete training, as well as in examinations .They are also trained to carry out workplace consultations in police stations. This project is successful, students are working much more effectively and the awareness of dyslexia throughout the whole organization is improving. It is being considered by other police services nationally and internationally.

Individual Case Study Jack - the Fire Fighter

When Jack joined the fire service he had no idea he might be dyslexic. He had just worked hard all his life. In training he failed his assessment and a trainer suggested he might be dyslexic.

Jack's assessment revealed that he had very good thinking skills particularly nonverbal problem solving, but his literacy and memory skills were weak and he was diagnosed as dyslexic.

The following recommendations were made

Problem	Skill development	Adjustment
Slow reading	Speed comprehension	Extra time in examinations
Poor spelling in exams		Pictorial and verbal explanations accepted
Poor spelling in development folder	Personal dictionary	Hand held spell checker and Text help
Lack of clear and accurate communication	Speech therapy. Repetition to automatic level	Extra time to express himself in examinations
Memory and recall	Multi sensory memory strategies Use of pictures and symbols to help with training pack information	Dictaphone for personal memos and in training
Confidence	Specialist training to help develop his understanding of impact of dyslexia	Mentor
Failing to pass examinations		Extended training and probationary period

Outcome

Jack is now a competent fire-fighter. He is seen as one of the most dependable members in the team. Whenever a new piece of equipment arrives he is given it first, he takes it apart then puts it together again and then clearly explains to his team about how to use it.

Conclusion

Being dyslexic should not be a barrier to working in any occupation. Dyslexic people can bring a range of specific skills to a job as well as being hard working and determined. Their success depends on their understanding of their dyslexia and its impact, the understanding of the task demands of the job, and the understanding of those around them to provide appropriate support.

5.4 Appreciating and Making the Most of Strengths

Bonita Thomson

Dyslexia is often misunderstood in the workplace. Mention 'dyslexia' and many people think that it's just a problem with reading and writing. It is, of course much more than that. Adults with dyslexia may well have struggled learning to read and write; they may still take much longer over such tasks but they have often developed ingenious strategies to get around their difficulties. Dyslexic people, like others, have individual strengths and weaknesses. They are usually creative, often intuitive thinkers who can use their strengths to tackle tasks they would otherwise find difficult.

It is very important for dyslexic people to understand and use their own particular strengths. They may need help to identify these strengths and find creative ways of using them to overcome or get around any difficulties. Time spent on these aspects is an investment and will help to release potential which will be of benefit to both the individual and the organisation.

There are a number of strengths that are often associated with dyslexia. Of course, an individual will not have strengths in all of the following. This list can be used to help identify and develop strengths in each person that will help them in their job and benefit the organisation:

- Non-verbal reasoning particularly with visual-spatial and visual perception tasks. Problem solving.
- Visual memory. Visual, holistic or intuitive thinking.

- Creativity. Generating innovative ideas.

- Good oral expression.

- Perseverance, determination and motivation.

- Knowledge of preferred working styles. Using appropriate strategies.

- Good organisation skills.

- Good people skills. Encouragement, patience and empathy.

- Energy and enthusiasm.

The employer, the line manager and colleagues may need to focus positively on identifying strengths, particularly if the dyslexic employee is struggling with some tasks. Questions an employer can ask are:

Can the task be done differently?

Does it need to be done at all?

Can it be done by another person, thus freeing up their time for something more creative, more visual?

Some Examples of Adapting Tasks to use Strengths

Instructions for using equipment are often written in a way that makes assumptions about a person's knowledge, or include lots of unfamiliar or similar words. This can be bad news for a dyslexic person. Try showing them how to use the equipment in a real situation. Let them go through it with you again, writing the instructions in their own words or capturing their own words on tape. They can then go away and devise their own instructions, with illustrations perhaps, and helpful hints. Then they can check them over with someone who is a proficient user. The new instructions may be even better than the original, more useful to others, for example, anyone for whom English is not their first language or a technophobe.

Complicated or formal procedures can be dealt with in a similar way. Do not underestimate the value of understanding the reason for any procedures. Dyslexic people find it difficult to work 'in the dark'.

They need to understand what they are doing and where it is leading. It helps them to remember.

Many dyslexic people are very articulate. They can express themselves very well when they are not having to think about punctuation, spelling, forming letters on the page. This ability can be tapped using other people or technology or both. A digital recorder is an excellent way of capturing words and ideas, capturing them at the instant of generation. Leaving the recorder to run is better than trying to dictate. The recording can then be typed up or given to someone else to type up and knock into shape. Once someone gets used to this way of getting ideas down, then they may like to move on to voice recognition software which takes the words as they are spoken and converts them into text in Word.

It is important that all employees are given encouragement, praise and sensitive positive feedback for the work they do, but this is vital for those with dyslexia because of their history of perceived failure, ridicule and bullying that may have been encountered at home, at school or in previous employment.

Workplace systems and procedures can often tap areas that dyslexic people find difficult. They usually have difficulty with tasks that put a heavy load on working memory. Instructions should be explicit, unambiguous; reasons and expected outcomes need to be explained.

Using Strengths - a Checklist

The following ideas have been developed with dyslexic people. It is not an exhaustive list. The suggestions can be adapted, new ones added to suit the task and the individual and the team.

Working Using Visual Strengths

- Mind maps, flowcharts and diagrams are useful for presenting instructions and procedures in a visual way. These can be A4 (or folded A3) size for including in reference files or larger for use as posters - other employees may find these useful too!

- Colour coding can be used to identify particular topics, subjects or projects, keeping folders, labels, post-its highlighters etc. in one colour for each area.

- Diagrams can be used as a starting point when staff or managers need to discuss or explain things.

- Use 'post-its' for temporary labels to aid memory.

- Formatting text in reports etc. should be broken up with sub-headings and bullet points. Pictures and diagrams should be included wherever possible as these help with visual recall.

Working using Auditory Strengths

- A small digital recorder is a valuable tool. The employee can:

- Capture their ideas instantly for inclusion in written material.

- Rehearse what they want to write or say before committing to paper or before attending a meeting.

■ Record reading text and then listen when checking work.

■ Work with music through headphones as an aid to concentration. Use recorded books or use read-back software.

■ Make up chants or songs for things that need remembering.

Working through Doing

■ Many people need to go through procedures at least once to check they have understood the task and the expected outcome. Dyslexic people may need to do this more than once and also write out procedures in their own way.

■ 'Walking through' procedures in a safe, encouraging environment. This is a form of role play. On their own they can dramatise scenes, act things out, to test how things will work or to help learn tasks.

Interacting with the Information by

■ Asking questions.

■ Preparing a diagram, flow chart or mind map.

■ Putting ideas or information onto index cards - doing this helps.

■ Using a computer programme like *Thinksheet* or *Inspiration* to plan.

■ Cutting up photocopies of relevant part of texts or newspaper articles and make a file.

■ Walking about while thinking.

■ Taking regular breaks is very important and preferably doing something physical in them to give the brain a rest.

Support and technology can be provided through the
Access to Work scheme:

■ Visual planning software such as *Inspiration* and *Spark-Space* which taps visual strengths for planning. The software can also be used to create flow charts and other useful diagrams.

■ Laptop to enable a person to work when away from their own workstation, working at home or on courses. Where security is an issue, it may be better to consider an *AlphaSmart*. This is a robust portable word processor which can be connected later to the office PC.

■ Some one-to-one specialist tuition to help develop strategies for the workplace using strengths. This should be delivered in a programme that is multi-sensory, structured and cumulative.

Bonita Thomson is a Practitioner and Consultant in Adult Dyslexia. She is co-author with Vicki Goodwin of 'Making Dyslexia Work for You', a self-help book for dyslexic adults and young people. The book includes several chapters of useful strategies and a chapter (Looking Wider) which addresses how others can help.

5.5 Identifying Skills for Work and Career Guidance

Steve O'Brien, Adult Dyslexia Access, British Dyslexia Association Organisational Member

To ensure dyslexic adults develop the skills to enable them to reach their full potential requires a tailored approach; focused on the individual's own traits, their strengths and weaknesses. Each adult has to be treated as an individual, each case of dyslexia being like a thumb print, unique and different. After 10 years of being an advocate and the Chief Executive of Adult Dyslexia Access (ADA) I have yet to see two identical dyslexic adults. Therefore it is illogical to suggest that a prescriptive approach is feasible or cost efficient; it cannot be prescriptive or 'off the peg'. Furthermore, Dyslexia support professionals need to expend time, effort and research to tailor the support to the dyslexic individual and the needs and job requirements. Therefore, employers need to question what interventions will enable their employee to function successfully in the workplace. Current legislation, such as the Disability Discrimination Act (DDA) or Disability Equality Duty (DED), does not arguably address the needs of their existing or prospective staff. However, it can be argued that current resources, research and services are biased towards education and children, rather than adults. The focus is on 'fixing' levels of literacy rather than a disability that affects short-term/working memory, organisational skills etc.

Young explains this issue precisely by stating:

The crux of the problem is that in the research, and interventions for adults, the issues that are addressed relate to LD/dyslexia from the perspective of children with reading problems, when

we should be approaching issues from the perspective of adults with disabilities, therefore we end up using the wrong intervention models for the population. (Young 2004)

The current reasonable adjustment for adults in employment is geared towards the use of assistive technology, funded through a grant scheme run by Job Centre Plus. The technology approach of prescriptive support is outdated, neither cost effective nor sufficient and results in a well intentioned but substantial waste of public funding. The development of vocational support strategies is paramount; the process of assessment needs to be focused on the needs of the individual in employment. The worlds of education and employment are strikingly dissimilar in this regard and the transitional phase from one to the other requires a greater focus in investment and development.

Universities and colleges adhere to disability legislation, the same cannot be said for all employers, and the world of work is notably a different experience, almost harsh. The university seeks to provide and support the student, the student's relationship with the university is like that of a patient in the NHS due to their duty of care. The student, whilst at university will potentially have access to a scribe, dictaphone to record lectures/meetings, computer software or laptop etc. However, when the student enters the world of employment there is little if any of this support made available to them. The grant process of support in employment is stigmatised by the Jobcentre Plus due to the nature of dyslexia being a hidden disability, and thus hinders the reasonable adjustment process. Little training is undertaken by job centres and the Department of Work and Pensions (DWP) to understand the needs of the dyslexic adult in employment or prospective employment. The sub contracted staff delivering support are also not qualified in the field of adult dyslexia support, most have specialised in a variety of disabilities and lack accredited qualifications in the field to successfully implement reasonable adjustments in the workplace.

Ignorance hinders dyslexics, over simplistic or even a wrong diagnosis and inappropriate support is a waste of time and potentially money. It is important not to set the adult up to fail through inappropriate support otherwise this has a long term detrimental effect on the confidence and self esteem of the dyslexic adult. Career guidance needs to be structured to the individual dyslexic adult.

These systemic failures ultimately lead to social alienation: which could include the opting out of education and employment. Research carried out by the ADA 2001-2004 in Merseyside has highlighted that 41% of the unemployed sampled were dyslexic. This research highlighted the need for support for adults in employment and vocational training to prevent them from becoming added to unemployment figures. It also emphasised the importance of appropriate support within welfare programs, in order to enable those who had become unemployed to gain the confidence and ability to access employment opportunities. If the individual's confidence and esteem are continually knocked then the person may become dysfunctional and this dysfunction is damaging to the individual. This has a social cost to tax payers and society.

Reasonable adjustments do not have to be complicated, many of the unemployed participants in the ADA's research merely wanted a driving licence and with the correct intervention many gained driving licences and fork lift truck licences. There were simple adjustments made such as a verbal test or voice activated software to read the driving theory. Once the test was passed they could get driving jobs or fork lift driving jobs and needed no further intervention. Dyslexics are often mistakenly offered the 'sticking plaster' of a computer, screen reader and voice input system. Whether in education or employment the solution is the same with the odd variation in the type of software. Technologies are important, it is what enables me to communicate as a dyslexic adult, but it is not the solution for all.

The need for quality intervention is critical, for example, a client who was a librarian was given the usual package of hardware and software and training from Access to Work (AtW), following £4000 worth of support, little or no improvement was made so the Librarian was referred to our organisation where he was assessed and given a vocational plan to address his problems. The assessment was the key to his success; it identified his strengths and weaknesses and enabled the individual to address his needs by practical solutions. His biggest problem was his short term memory and a simple note book and pencil were adopted to help improve his memory, the note pad becoming his short term memory, added to this was a simple list of 'things to do' and the ability to keep rough notes became the practical solution for this individual. The line manager would write in the note pad a list of work duties and both were happy, since intervention the client has positive work reviews and is content within their employment.

Professionals in the field of adult dyslexia support need to keep up to date with the latest technological advancements or specialties in this specific field. The internet is a great source of informative solutions; there are useful websites, blogs and conferences that inform the professionals on the latest support and information available. I was recently sitting in a university that was using Text Help Version 4 and Dragon Naturally Speaking 5, I mentioned that both programmes have since advanced into versions of double figures to the amazement of the dyslexia coordinator. Keeping up to date with technology advancements is important, new features, accuracy and cost can make technology more beneficial to the user.

The standard dyslexia assessment is not appropriate for employment; it is designed and implemented to inform educationalists of the individual's cognitive performance. In employment the interpreter usually does not have the skills to decipher the report and make a judgment as to what to do next. Assessment cannot be received through the letter box for the individual or employer to decipher; they have to be written in plain English and accessible to the dyslexic adult. The ADA helpline frequently receives phone enquiries from employers, parents or dyslexic adults to explain educational psychologists' reports. Reports need to be tailored to the individual and have a strong vocational element. A four page report with I.Q. scores and reading ages are not appropriate in employment, greater detail of cognitive weaknesses and strengths need to be explored to enable an informative individual work plan. This work plan should include educational and vocational development, it also a needs assessment and a glossary. The work plan must be fed back by an experienced practitioner, who can explain the vocational assessment and enable the individual to take ownership of their dyslexia, and offer the appropriate support.

As a specialised adult orientated organisation the ADA devised such a process for the dyslexic adults and employment market in partnership with the Learning and Skills Council to address the needs of their cohort of learners and employers. The ADA delivers a fully accredited training package to train employers and service providers such as Remploy, local authorities and police authorities and we offer vocational support to address the needs of dyslexics, which is based on solid research collated over the last 10 years via supporting adults and employers.

Guidance in the field of dyslexia and employment should be intrinsically linked to education either secondary or further and higher. Service providers of information, advice and guidance (IAG) should embrace training and incorporate learning disabilities / dyslexia training as part of their professional development and matrix of the qualification of IAG , so the Connexions Service and the like can incorporate support to assist in the transition of adults into the employment field.

Organisational approach needs to accept that educational solutions are not appropriate and can even be counterproductive in employment. Technologies have to be appropriate, sometimes solutions have to have an element of innovation, perseverance and could be simply a process of trial and error. Employers need to develop strategies to address the needs of the diverse workforce, human resources departments need to embrace change and develop policy and strategies to enhance their service to the dyslexic adult. The organisation has the responsibility to accept the legitimacy of dyslexia and acknowledge its hidden nature as a disability. The notion of making reasonable adjustments needs to be encouraged and the ethos of 'fixing' the adult's literacy needs to be acknowledged to often be inappropriate. Dyslexics don't need a quick fix, a cure or a space hopper, more understanding and acceptance is needed for success.

The dyslexic adult needs access to efficient identification through psychometric dyslexia screening and appropriate dyslexia vocationally based assessments that are consumer friendly. The identification also needs to empower the individual to understand their disability and enable them to advocate on their own behalf, knowing what steps are necessary to access appropriate reasonable adjustments and the ability to know one's legal rights in employment. The access to identification also needs to be funded freely by the DWP or the responsibility of the employers under disability legislation, such as the DED or DDA.

The fundamental structure is in place to deliver the service required by dyslexics to gain the skills required to compete equally in employment. The correct investment in training employers and service providers to identify and support dyslexic adults in the workplace is important to empower the individual to reach their full potential. This cost is miniscule compared to the investment in keeping a dyslexic adult in prison, on welfare payments or as part of the NEET population.

5.6 Supporting Dyslexic Employees

Ellen Morgan

Increased awareness that dyslexic children grow into dyslexic adults has underpinned provision for specialist dyslexia support in further and higher education. The next leap is to recognise that dyslexic individuals leave education and enter the world of work. For those who have identified their strengths early on, the choice of employment may reflect their entrepreneurial or creative talents. Many dyslexic people pursue careers in the arts (ranging from music through art, drama, architecture and journalism), while others may become self-employed and express their talents in fields such as catering, carpentry or other areas that demand 'practical' skills. Still other dyslexic individuals enter more traditional professions such as teaching, social work, law, nursing, and related medical fields.

In fact, the range of jobs available to dyslexic adults is the same as that open to non-dyslexic adults. However, dyslexic employees may require some accommodations to enable them to fulfil their potential at work. Fortunately, the Disability Discrimination Act (2005) covers people with Specific Learning Difficulties and makes it incumbent upon employers to provide reasonable adjustments to address their disability-related needs. Support may involve recognition of weaknesses such as slow reading speed, inaccurate spelling, weak punctuation and possible organisational difficulties, particularly in relation to time management and multi-tasking. The intention of this article is to suggest ways in which employers might utilise some tried and trusted learning strategies that dyslexic students often employ in educational settings, but which are equally beneficial in the workplace.

The nature of Specific Learning Difficulties such as dyslexia and dyspraxia varies from individual to individual, with the particular profile determined through a diagnostic assessment. It is therefore essential to identify the areas in a specific job that might pose problems for the individual dyslexic employee. For example, someone might be a top chef, but find it difficult to write out a daily menu as a result of weak spelling. Someone else might find that slow processing speed necessitates spending more time reading and/or writing reports. Others might need support in prioritising tasks or taking down accurate phone messages. The list of job tasks is endless, and consequently it is important not to make assumptions about what an individual finds difficult, but rather to talk to the employee and identify what aspects of the job are challenging.

Although there are many learning strategies from which dyslexic individuals can benefit, it is crucial not to place the main emphasis on 'problems' and 'difficulties' faced by dyslexic employees. Of equal importance are the positive contributions that many dyslexic people bring to the workplace. Often, though not always, those with 'right-brained' learning styles are able to see the big picture, work well as team members and may offer creative solutions to challenges faced by the companies for whom they work. Their innovative ideas present a fresh perspective in the workplace, where they may contribute orally what they find difficult to convey in writing.

There are several general learning principles that apply to many dyslexic individuals and suggest strategies that might be adapted to appropriate situations at work.

Specific learning difficulties are usually characterised by problems processing information, a weakness in short-term auditory or visual memory and sequencing difficulties. Some people may find it difficult to absorb information presented aurally; others may find it difficult to access information presented only in written form. For such individuals, effective learning is significantly aided by presenting information in a multi-sensory way. Information is more likely to 'go in' and be recalled if it is presented through auditory and visual means. Motor memory also plays a large part in learning and retaining knowledge, and many dyslexic people state that they learn best by doing.

Whenever possible, new tasks should be explained, modelled, tried by the learner and reinforced through visual information, such as a drawing or diagram in addition to written instructions. Take, for example, the task of using a piece of office equipment such as a photocopier. This might be challenging to someone who is not familiar with the procedures. Simply presenting the manual is most likely not the best way to overcome an employee's anxiety about mastering what may be an expected part of the job.

A more effective approach would be to demonstrate the required procedures, talking them through as they are performed. This could be followed by a practical session in which the employee tries out the task and has the opportunity to ask questions. A simple handout that sets out the task visually and includes a step-by-step explanation of what needs to be done will reinforce the learning. Although this may appear to be a lot of trouble to go through for one employee, it will, of course, make the task easier for all employees to learn and therefore increase the general efficiency of all staff. Although non-dyslexic employees may find it easier than dyslexic people to master certain aspects of learning, using multi-sensory approaches will nonetheless help all staff to learn more effectively.

In considering multi-sensory approaches to teaching new skills on-the-job, visual markers are a powerful tool to aid learning, recall and structuring and managing tasks and time. For example, one way to help a dyslexic employee prioritise various activities at work is to agree a colour code and then use it to represent the relative importance of different tasks. A green marker may signify something that is 'ready to go', whereas red could be used for urgent material requiring immediate attention. Yellow might reflect work that is in progress, but needs additional input before it can be progressed. Reusable coloured sticky tabs can be inserted at the appropriate point in a document. Putting work in trays of the agreed colour might also help to prioritise, by ensuring that the employee knows which tasks must be attended to first, and which are of less importance.

Many dyslexic and dyspraxic individuals have benefited from living in a technological age; computers with special software such as speech to text recognition, text reading and spell checkers, digital recorders, and personal organisers may provide immeasurable advantages for dyslexic people. For some, the confidence gained through the advances in technology have enabled them to access education and gain skills that formerly might not have been possible. In some cases, a work-based needs assessment may identify relevant software that can help an individual perform the job more effectively, and the employer can then put into place the necessary reasonable adjustments.

Many dyslexic people have developed their own strategies to help them cope with the more challenging aspects of their work lives. These may have no apparent impact on their work, but are essential coping strategies. For example, a successful head of a building company took digital photos of a prospective job to use as a reminder of what was required, and referred back to them when drawing up his estimate. Although he struggled with reading and writing, his ability to see the big picture enabled him to orchestrate the execution of a job. He knew when and how to employ appropriate specialists to undertake the carpentry, plumbing, wiring, etc. His itemised breakdown of the tasks involved and the relevant costs were presented on a clearly laid out word-processed document. What was his strategy for doing this when he was not himself a confident writer? Simple: he dictated the job specifications and costs to his wife, who used her computer knowledge to present an impressive document, and the client was won over.

Employers must approach the needs of their dyslexic and dyspraxic staff with sensitivity and understanding; by identifying areas where an individual may need some support and discussing how best to implement the support, the employee will be helped to overcome any anxiety relating to his or her ability to fulfil the job specifications, and the employer will benefit from the strengths, knowledge and creative input which the employee brings to the job.

Summary of Points

- Specific Learning Difficulties such as dyslexia and dyspraxia are recognised disabilities under the Disability Discrimination Act 2005.

- Employers are legally obliged to make appropriate reasonable adjustments to accommodate the needs of dyslexic and dyspraxic employees.

- Employers should talk to the employee and identify potential challenging aspects of the job to enable joint discussion of where adjustments might be necessary.

- Learning is most effective if information is presented in a multi-sensory way.

- Advances in technology can provide immeasurable benefits to a dyslexic employee.

- Dyslexic employees often bring creative and lateral problem-solving abilities to their jobs and these may be beneficial to their employers.

Ellen is currently a Specialist Dyslexia Assessor at The City University, London. She is a member of the SpLD Assessment Standards Committee (SASC) set up by the Department of Industry, Universities and Skills (DIUS) to address issues of standardising diagnostic assessments for students with Specific Learning Difficulties. She was also a founder member of the national Association of Dyslexia Specialists in Higher Education (ADSHE). Ellen has written books and articles and lectured widely on issues affecting dyslexic adults.

5.7 Case Study

Vicki McNicol, BDA Trainer

I discovered quite late in life that I was dyslexic. I couldn't believe it at the time and I don't know what shocked me the most - the fact that I was dyslexic or the fact that I had an extremely high IQ. This knowledge was empowering, I was able to take control of my dyslexia and be responsible for it. I learned to work in a different way and began a journey of discovery. My confidence and self-esteem significantly improved although I still have that little voice in my head, when approaching something new, that immediately tells me that I can't do it, I am now able to lower the volume of that voice and use my new skills to tackle the new task.

I was fundraising director at the British Dyslexia Association at the time of my discovering I was dyslexic. I began to see my dyslexia as a gift because it's my strengths; excellent communication skills, good problem solving skills, great lateral and strategic thinking skills and being a people person, that have enabled me to succeed. I have become passionate about dyslexia and about helping those with it to find a way forward so that they too can overcome the barriers it presents.

I had a successful career at the BDA but in March 2008 I was able to start up my own dyslexia-awareness training agency - Dyslexia Awareness UK. I am now a qualified trainer and use the knowledge and experience I have gained to improve the way children, young people and adults are taught and how dyslexic employees are supported. I am now also able to coach dyslexic adults and parents so that they can find a new way forward.

My life seems to have gone full circle and I am now doing a job that is varied, challenging and deeply satisfying. My headmistress said to me on my last day at school 'you have wasted your entire school career and my time, you are not even good enough to be a lavatory attendant' - I just wish she could see me now!!

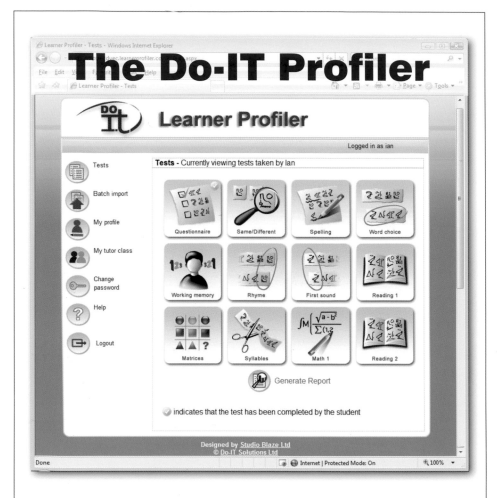

The Do-IT Profiler

The **Do-IT Profiler** – an online tool for identification of individual strengths and difficulties including reading, spelling and maths difficulties. It can be an "out of the box" solution or it can be tailored for your specific needs.

For details and a free trial contact
info@learnerprofiler.co.uk

5.8 Raising Self-Esteem

Vicki Godwin

Encouraging and praising others for the things they do well is not something most of us do enough at home or in the workplace. It is particularly important for dyslexic individuals who will have had to work literally twice as hard as others to do particular tasks.

Why Self-Esteem may be Particularly Fragile

Many dyslexic adults will have had a hard time at school because their difficulties are often centred on acquiring fluency in reading which dominates so much of the learning process in education.

They may have been criticised for apparently not trying because their performance seems at variance with other skills they clearly possess. Their families too may have expressed more frustration and criticism than understanding and support. They may have come to believe that they are not competent in many ways rather than in certain specific areas.

All this is very frustrating for the individual. Some people have described it as feeling rather like competing in a series of different matches say a swimming race, a running race and so on. They are doing well until they reach for example the tennis match. Then they find the task incredibly hard. It feels as if they have been given a squash racquet to use instead of a tennis racquet and of course it is impossible for them to perform as well. Moreover no-one else seems to be aware that they have a different and inappropriate tool: they may not always know it themselves. They may only be aware that the task is really suddenly much harder and that they and others around them are frustrated by their sudden dip in performance.

This is why dyslexia is often described as a 'hidden' disability.

We all have days when, under pressure or feeling a bit off-colour, we make mistakes, but this can happen much more often for someone with dyslexia. Dead-lines and sudden unexpected or unfamiliar requirements can 'throw' someone with dyslexia more easily, usually because their short-term memory is not as efficient as their long-term memory. One dyslexic adult described how they managed to prepare all their papers at home for an important meeting and then managed to leave them behind in their haste to get in on time. Following directions to get to a new meeting place or building, can absorb more energy than the activity that follows getting there.

Often a dyslexic adult will have developed all sorts of useful coping strategies but the fear of being caught out, of being taken by surprise, or simply feeling overwhelmed is never far away.

Previous bad experiences may have increased feelings of not being understood, of humiliation and low self-esteem.

How to Support Self Esteem

DO:

- Be patient and understanding - your confidence that they will get there is crucial and acts like the opposite of pressure.

- Give clear instructions - avoid rushed explanations as you head out of the door! A dyslexic adult may find following the instructions for working the photo-copier machine in order to print off an innovative piece of work more difficult than the work itself.

- Provide a work-map of the office, where staff normally sit etc. It feels embarrassing to not be able to retain what other people regard as simple information like a code or a name and it is so difficult to cope when you don't know.

- Ask existing staff to update useful sheets of information or FAQ's (frequently asked questions) that a new employee can refer to on various procedures so that they do not have to ask the same question all the time.

- Allocate every new employee an understanding mentor - on the same grade so they can easily ask general questions (and who will be naturally patient and helpful when a simple procedure needs repeating again).

- Give time slots for a dyslexic employee to make their own notes etc. to cope with office/work practice.

- Where appropriate offer small group presentation half-hours - some dyslexic employees will pick up even more quickly from a spoken presentation by colleagues describing what they do - this too may benefit all the team.

- Give debriefing sessions to ask what would be most useful to enable them to work more efficiently (again good for all employees) and identify which difficulties in their dyslexia are causing most aggravation in their work.

- Do support their IT and the provision of useful software they may have used before.

- Find time to provide overviews of work beforehand (of each week or month or set of tasks) Many people will thrive on working from the whole picture to the particular task and often provide new and valuable insights into the work to be done.

■ Give responsibility for individual work so that they can do some work independently and in their own way.

■ Offer genuine encouragement and praise whenever possible - and there will be many opportunities.

■ Offer them opportunities to demonstrate their skills - working to their strengths. The tasks that are most difficult, ironically, will be the ones an employer may consider hardly worth a mention.

DON'T:

■ Make 'oh didn't I tell you that?' type of remarks that unintentionally highlight their area of difficulty.

■ Put people on the spot. Wherever possible - give warning - for a new task to allow for preparation time. Being put on the spot is something most people feel uncomfortable about. For someone with dyslexia that challenge is worse, especially if it involves a lot of rapid reading whereas they may be the best at responding quickly and creatively in spoken discussions. They will do the reading - but need time.

■ Announce their dyslexia to others but check with them what approach they would prefer. Just as no one would introduce a colleague as 'our blind colleague here' the same is true for all disabilities.

Work situations are stressful and busy for everyone so it isn't easy to find time to bring out the best in everyone but it really pays off. Some dyslexic adults are quite bruised by past negative experiences in education and some aspects of daily life. The feeling that they are valued for the contributions they make may have been all too rare an experience in the past. There are many studies which show how much better and how much more productively everyone works in an atmosphere of trust and encouragement - this is even more the case for someone with dyslexia.

As with everyone - look for strengths - they will be there! And tell people!

5.9 Dyslexia: the Line Manager's Challenge.

Katherine Kindersley, Dyslexia Assessment and Consultancy, British Dyslexia Association Organisational Member

This article looks at how dyslexia can cause particular challenges for line managers and, using a case study, shows how these may be resolved.

The first point to note is that while people with dyslexia may bring exceptional gifts and skills to their work, dyslexia can also be the reason for underperformance in all sectors and across all levels of employment. Yet the employee's dyslexia may not be recognised. There are a number of reasons for this.

- Dyslexia is a 'hidden' disability.

- The line manager may not know about dyslexia.

- The line manager may understand dyslexia to be a problem only with spelling and reading.

- The employee may not know that he has dyslexia, and is bewildered as to where the problems lie, or what might help.

- The employee was successful in his previous role, so the current difficulties are perplexing.

- The employee may have chosen not to reveal his dyslexia to his employer.

- There may be knowledge of the employee's dyslexia, but there is a lack of information on what may be done to help.

In a typical situation, the employee is working long hours, but targets are not being met. The line manager's frustrations are intensified by the seeming inability of the employee to respond to the additional support and monitoring which has been given. The employee is unable to explain why he is not able to improve. (In this article, he is used to refer to the employee and she to refer to the line manager).

Stuart: A Challenging Employee

Stuart was not just a challenge: Lisa, his line manager, found him exasperating! He had been moved into her team three months previously, arriving with good references from his manager. He was employed as an Insurance Sales Consultant and his job was to provide home insurance quotations to customers over the telephone and to meet sales performance targets.

Stuart certainly put in the hours and was hard-working. Lisa, recognising this, had supported him by providing some additional one-to-one 'catch-up' sessions. Yet there had been no significant improvement. She listed his problems.

Stuart was

- Slow to learn new product information;
- Unable to remember consistently the recent updates in product information;
- Slow to find the appropriate information on the company database.

Furthermore

- When speaking on the telephone, he seemed to lose track of where he was, and go over information unnecessarily;

- He sometimes omitted important questions;

- He took too long to log the information following a call;

- He was not accurate when entering client information onto the database;

- His emails were unclear.

Lisa felt she had given Stuart plenty of support. She now had no alternative but to place him on a capability review process, with formal monitoring of performance. As a result, Stuart's anxiety increased, as he feared he would not receive his bonuses and might even lose his job.

> When an employee is not performing to expectations, it is important to consider whether the person may have an unidentified 'hidden' disability.

A Common Situation

These circumstances are not unusual. We frequently meet situations similar to that of Lisa and Stuart across the whole range of employment sectors, where in spite of the individual being apparently well-motivated and hard-working, and the line manager wishing to be supportive, performance issues remain. Anxiety and stress on the part of the employee exacerbate the situation.

The relationship between the employer and employee deteriorates. Difficulties are not understood by the line manager, nor, as in the case of Stuart, by the employee himself. Tensions grow and conflicts multiply.

Dyslexia is a Complex Condition

A difficulty for the Line Manager is that dyslexia often appears to be an amorphous, and therefore perplexing condition. It manifests in many different ways, depending on the intricate patterning of a person's abilities, training, skills, experience, personality, and the demands made on the individual. Dyslexia can also be more difficult to recognise in adults, as they may well have developed compensatory strategies in some areas, or have concealed their difficulties in others.

In the work environment, the person with dyslexia is likely to meet the greatest challenges in the following three areas: memory, the ability to recall and hold onto information in the short-term; organisation, the ability to remain in control of activity and time, and thirdly, the ability to work with speed and accuracy.

Thus difficulties may be seen across a whole range of work tasks which are dependent on the efficient processing of information.

The Challenge of the Workplace

Recent trends in the workplace have tended to increase the difficulties experienced by employees with dyslexia.

Workplaces have become more pressurised; performance targets and performance monitoring are increasingly common.

Employees are expected to work to short timescales and tight deadlines.

In addition, workplaces commonly demand the following:

- Accurate literacy.

- Multi-tasking skills.

- The strict following of a procedure: the way a task is completed is considered as important as the result.

Further challenges in the workplace, perhaps especially for new entrants, may be created because, in contrast to the world of education, help is often given only if it is requested or if there are performance problems. Also workplace relationships are normally long-term and employees cannot choose their workplace colleagues, which may create friction.

In the context of the demands described above, a change of circumstances at work often puts additional pressure on an employee and this may be the reason for the dyslexic difficulties being revealed. The pressures may be a change of job, or a promotion, bringing new and challenging responsibilities. There may be a new line manager who introduces a different style of management and different ways of working. A new appraisal system may record performance in a more detailed way.

More monitoring and supervision can highlight weak performance.

It may be that a change in personnel results in the dyslexic person losing a particularly supportive colleague. Perhaps even a change in a personal relationship means that there is no longer someone outside work who can check documents for the employee. Change can affect both the work performance and the emotional well-being of an employee with dyslexia.

> The line manager should consider if a recent change
> has affected the performance of an employee.

How Stuart's Situation was Resolved

Stuart had talked to friends about his worries at work, and it was they who suggested that he contact Human Resources and raise the possibility that he might have dyslexia. This was something he had not considered before, and faced with the looming capability procedure, he plucked up courage to speak to his manager. As a result, he was referred for a dyslexia assessment and following this, a workplace needs assessment. Both of these assessments were important in helping Stuart become effective in his role, and I now look at these in more detail.

The Diagnostic Assessment

The diagnostic assessment confirmed that Stuart had some elements of dyslexia combined with a condition called dyspraxia. Stuart himself felt a sense of huge relief that the cause of his difficulties was understood. He was also very reassured to learn that in some areas he was highly gifted; his verbal reasoning ability, he was told, placed him in the 'very superior' range of his age group in the general population. Yet in contrast, he had low scores in tests which tap the ability to process visual information and there were also weaknesses with working memory and with attention.

> When dyslexia is identified, the solutions become clearer. The tensions between the line manager and the employee subside.

As Stuart's case exemplified, the 'diagnostic' assessment enables the employee's profile to be properly understood and it is therefore important for a number of reasons. The line manager can see why workplace adjustments should be made. The workplace assessor can identify the particular ways in which the employee can be supported, as well as how much support is likely to be needed.

It also becomes clear where the emphasis of the skills training should be placed, and thus the assessment provides important information for a specialist trainer.

The information provided by the diagnostic assessment may also make all the difference to a person's career and life. At the very least, it should ensure that the recommendations made are realistic and appropriate for the individual employee. However, I also know of cases where it has enabled the employee to recognise that he is in the wrong job, resulting in a change of career and success in a new field.

The Workplace Needs Assessment

The assessor explored the different aspects of Stuart's job and made particular recommendations in the form of assistive software, equipment and individual specialist training. (For more detailed information see the article in this Handbook on the Workplace Needs Assessment, see Chapter 2.6) by Sylvia Moody.

It is sometimes possible to make adjustments to the job itself.

In Stuart's case, he was able to move from a position in the 'Inbound' Calls Department to the adjacent 'Outbound' Calls Department. In his new role, he made calls to existing customers and he was therefore able to check the profile of the customer, and prepare the information he needed in advance of making the call. With such preparation, he found he could use his verbal strengths more effectively.

Support for the Line Manager

People cannot work successfully in isolation. Stuart was unable to sort out his difficulties by himself. Lisa too needed the input of Human Resources and her managers to resolve the issues surrounding Stuart's performance. Yet the perspective needs to be wider. The most supportive and productive workplaces are those where training has created an awareness of dyslexia and related conditions throughout the organisation. There is an understanding that people may need to work differently. People are enabled to work with their strengths, and adjustments are accepted as part of the workplace culture.

Further Reading

Dyslexia and Employment: A Guide for Assessors, Trainers and Managers. Edited by Sylvia Moody. Wiley-Blackwell 2009.

www.workingwithdyslexia.com and the information sheets under:

http://www.dyslexiaassessmentandconsultancy.co.uk/info-sheets.php

5.10 Towards inclusive Practice in the Workplace

Nicky Martin

I know a second year history student at a Russell Group university. He is an able writer and in demand to produce pieces for the university newspaper on a regular basis. This young man's dream is to become a journalist and logically his next move will be an MA in Journalism. With a lively mind, successful writing experience, a keen journalistic style, grade A at A level in English Literature and, eventually, very probably, a good degree, the ambition is realistic. He is however, sadly, not even going down that road because once, in the first year, a lecturer made an insensitive comment about spelling during a 'fun' end-of-term quiz activity which involved hand written responses. Journalists write in a notebook, someone might see. Assistive technology can refine the finished article, but the notebook might let him down and he is acutely sensitive, and feels too stigmatised to take the risk. There was a moment when things could have gone either way. If the lecturer had kept his insensitive comments to himself, the world could potentially have benefited from a gifted and original journalist. He didn't and the result is further damage to self esteem and the erection of an unnecessary barrier which is likely to thwart the achievement of considerable potential.

The negative impact of dyslexia on self esteem is well documented (Burden 2008, Humphrey 2003, Pollak 2005, Ridsdale 2004, Singer 2008).The life experience of older people with dyslexia may include failing the eleven plus exam and embarking at that tender age on a form of segregated education for those deemed to be less intelligent, with all the limitations to employment choices that this implies. University students are frequently identified as dyslexic during their first degree so diagnosis is often a recent and raw experience, and graduates may well enter the workplace with unresolved feelings, including acute self-consciousness (www.BRAIN-HE.com accessed 06-01-09, Pollak 2005).

Although there are those who are able to embrace and celebrate their neurodiversity, entering the world of work with a hangover of negativity and damaged self esteem is a reality for many people with dyslexia. The inclusive workplace is an environment which takes positive action to ameliorate the impact of earlier negative experiences, to celebrate diversity and to foster a sense of belonging in all employees. When the doughnuts are passed around with the coffee, no one would crack a joke at the expense of an overweight colleague. In the same way, a notebook of idiosyncratic spelling would not be worthy of comment. The British Workplace Behaviours Survey (2008), which involved almost 4000 workers, found 'harassment at work, including humiliation, low expectations and unfair criticism', to be a common experience for disabled people (www.equalityhumanrights.com, accessed 31-12-08).

In order to empathise with the experience, remember the last time you felt really humiliated, and consider how difficult you might find it to do your job while in the resulting emotional state.

This article adopts a Social Model stance in which people with impairments are deemed to be disabled by the obstacles they encounter in society. (Barnes 2004, Barton 2004, Oliver 2004).

The experience of attitudinal barriers is most frequently cited by disabled people (Gradwell 1997). A social model response would be to work with disabled colleagues in order to identify obstructions and find ways over, around, and through them.

The word 'impairment' is interesting in itself. Individuals who are positive about dyslexia as a neurodiverse way of being which brings with it a range of strengths including, critically, the ability to think strategically, and to see the bigger picture, may reject the term. Disabling negative attitudes may, however, have impacted on the life experience of even the most positive and resilient neurodiverse person (Pollak 2005).

Occupational standards which suggest that 'dyslexics' can't succeed in branches of the medical profession, for example, are inherently disabling if they stop an individual from accessing appropriate higher education (Dale and Aiken 2007, Hoong-Sin and Fong 2008, Murphy 2008). Fear of being discriminated against at work may well inhibit disclosure and therefore access to workplace reasonable adjustments (NIACE 2008). Arguably an insensitive remark or a misplaced joke at the expense of a 'bad speller' or someone 'incapable of telling left from right' could be as effective a deterrent to even trying as slamming a door in someone's face.

The inclusive workplace would ideally demonstrate an environment in which 'put downs' and day to day humiliations are not part of the culture and a level of sensitivity operates which enables everyone to do the best job they can. Perhaps addressing dyslexia typical barriers could lead to working practices which are beneficial to the organisation as a whole. This point is illustrated with a few examples which focus on the generic office context, but may well apply in a range of settings. The list presented is not intended to be exhaustive but is offered as a catalyst.

- Corridor conversations which absolve the imparter of the information of any responsibility to action whatever it was that was agreed, death by email, copying everyone in to everything whether they need to know or not, and similar practices, really need looking at for everyone's sake.

- An individual with dyslexia is very likely to experience short term memory problems (Grant 2007, Pollak 2005), as is someone who is highly stressed or anxious, and anyone not headed back to their office straight after the interaction occurred. Clearly eliminating this sort of corridor conversation is therefore helpful all round and not necessarily a dyslexia specific reasonable adjustment.

- Hands up who likes to receive over a hundred emails a day including over thirty which were just 'copying in' for no apparent reason? So-it's not just helpful for employees who have dyslexia then to inculcate the team into the culture of thinking before pressing send? That horrible rifling through a sea of papers for the right ones for the meeting could be solved by providing paper copies or sending them the day before, all in one email entitled 'papers needed for meeting x at 10 am on given date'.

- Who loves filing? Who has a filing system which is the same as another person's? Who is running out of space in the office? OK - it would be dyslexia friendly to get filing under control as a team - it would also be efficient and team friendly. How about working out a system in which each member of the team takes responsibility for one set of information for example? An overwhelming and inefficient task could be made manageable fairly simply, with a complete set of information in a central location which is regularly updated by a named individual, and backed up electronically.

- How many people didn't get all of the ICT instructions first time around and then struggled on feeling embarrassed about asking again? Who is embarrassed because they don't know which way up the paper goes in the fax machine - or the printer? Would you curl up and die if you screwed up all your courage to ask and the response was sarcasm - or a joke at your expense? A little bit of sensitivity at work could save an awful lot of embarrassment. Step-by-step instructions by the fax machine and using the same number of words to answer the question about how that bit of ICT works, rather than trashing the self esteem is always more productive.

Assistive technology, originally designed to support disabled people may well be of great benefit to whole teams. Networked access to appropriate software, and adequate training in its use, could enhance team efficiency and reduce risk of stigmatisation, of those identified by the software on their computer, as 'other'.

'Access to Work' is designed to help disabled people to make the best contribution possible to the workforce. Developments are proposed which will make the scheme more widely available. (www.dwp.gov.uk/noonewrittenoff, accessed 06-01-09) In an ideal world, a smooth progression, for example, from Disabled Student Allowance at University, to Access to Work in employment, would really help. Everyday inclusive practice in the workplace would certainly help everyone.

References

Barnes C (2004) *Disability ,disability studies and the academy* in Swain J, French S, Barnes C, Thomas C (eds) (2004) *Disabling barriers, enabling environments*. Sage. London.

Barton L (2004) *The Disability Movement: Some observations.* in Swain J, French S, Barnes C, Thomas C (eds) (2004) *Disabling barriers, enabling environments.* Sage. London.

Burden R (2008) *Is dyslexia necessarily associated with negative feelings of self worth? A review and implications for further research.* Dyslexia 14 (3) 188-196. John Wiley and Sons.

Dale C, Aiken F (2007) *A review of the literature into dyslexia in nursing practice.* Royal College of Nursing. Practice Education Forum.

www.dwp.gov.uk (2008) *Consultation on welfare reform ends'* DWP Media Centre 24th October 2008.

Equality and Human Rights Commission (2008) British workplace behaviour survey 2008. Equality News www.equalityhumanrights.com accessed 31-12-08.

Gradwell L (1998) *A rose by any other name. Healthmatters* (32) Winter 1997/8 8-9.

Grant D (2007) *Neurodiversity :Diagnostic issues in higher education.* NADP Technical Briefing 3/2007.

Hoong-Sin C, Fong J (2008) *The impact of regulatory fitness requirements on disabled social work students.* British Journal of Social Work on line May 31st 2008. 1-22. Oxford University Press.

Humphrey N (2003) *Teacher and pupil ratings of self esteem in developmental dyslexia.* British Journal of Special Education 29 (1) 29-36.

Murphy F (2008) *The clinical experience of dyslexic healthcare students.* www.sciencedirect.com/science accessed 05-01-09.

NIACE (2008) *From compliance to culture change. Disabled staff working in lifelong learning.* NIACE. March 2008. Leicester.

Oliver M (2004) *If I had a hammer. The Social Model in action* in Swain J, French S, Barnes C, Thomas C (eds) (2004) Disabling barriers, enabling environments. Sage. London.

Pollak D (2005) *Dyslexia, the self and higher education. Learning life histories of students identified as dyslexic.* Trentham Books. Stoke on Trent.

Ridsdale J (2004) *Dyslexia and self esteem* in Turner M, Rack J (eds) *The study of dyslexia.* Springer US.

Singer E (2008) *Coping with academic failure. A study of Dutch children with dyslexia.* Dyslexia 14 (4) 314-333. John Wiley and Sons.

5.11 Dyslexia: Should Managers be Knowledgeable?

By Anne Kent

According to Andi Sanderson (2008), many businesses in the United Kingdom do not know how to recognise employees with dyslexia or how to support them. There seems to be a real lack of understanding of what it is to be dyslexic in the workplace or how to support people who have the condition. This is quite surprising considering that it is estimated that ten percent of the population have dyslexia to some degree, but then again dyslexia is a "hidden" problem. Many businesses therefore will have employees in their organisation who are dyslexic, even though they may not be aware of it.

With all this in mind, should all managers have knowledge of what dyslexia is and know how they can support dyslexics in their employment? The short answer to these questions is a definite "Yes". However, the short answer "Yes" is not going to convince anyone to learn the skills and so here is a longer answer in order to persuade employers to take this issue seriously.

There are numerous reasons why managers should have some knowledge of dyslexia. Above all, there is one obvious reason: some dyslexics are protected from discrimination practices under the Disability Discrimination Act (DDA. 1995/2005) and this act can help some people with dyslexia gain access to the workplace. Therefore, it is logical to suspect that some managers without any knowledge of dyslexia may be breaking the law as set out in the DDA. However, more importantly it seems to be a waste of the talents and abilities dyslexic employees can bring to businesses and it makes economic sense to maximise their contribution in these difficult financial times.

One problem is that most people do not comprehend what it is like to be dyslexic and understanding may hold the solution to taking the steps necessary to support employees. Being dyslexic can be like living in an alien world. Imagine what it would be like to live in a world where you did not understand anyone or were not able to interact effectively, because they are all talking in a language you do not comprehend. How would you feel in this kind of world? Well at the extreme some individuals with dyslexia feel this way and live in this sort of world every day of their life. They are shut out just because society fails to understand their dyslexic problems and support them. It is like asking a group of ten individuals to climb a steep hill and saying that the last three to reach the top would have to clean the toilets for a year. However, three of the individuals are made to wear roller skates and are blindfolded. It is obvious which three would be last. Therefore, would you consider it to be an inequitable race? Yet some people with dyslexia deal with this sort of injustice every day of their life and for this reason dyslexics are often restrained to low skilled jobs and fail to gain or keep promotion, a hidden form of discrimination that needs to be stopped.

The pressures of being dyslexic in a text based society can be extremely difficult on a daily basis when there is very little or no support or understanding available. Many dyslexics may feel systematically humiliated within the workplace by other staff and management simply because of their inability to work at the same speed, in the same way or for not having the same basic levels of understanding and literacy skills as other employees.

Some dyslexic weaknesses can define a dyslexic individual as being different, as not being normal, instead of allowing the individual to be treated with respect and encouragement. Dyslexia does not have to stop anyone from achieving their goals if there is understanding and support to achieve them.

Dyslexia is a learning disability, which involves difficulties with processing language even when someone seems very intelligent and is motivated to learn. It is not a disease, but is a condition that normally runs in families. Many dyslexics work very hard at hiding or at compensating for their learning difficulties, so it can be difficult to recognise. Some dyslexics are successful in their work despite their dyslexia difficulties and are well aware they need to work harder, longer hours and be determined to succeed. Many are non-linear thinkers, have powers of visualisation, excellent practical skills and have holistic ways of dealing with tasks which may not seem conventional to others.

You may be asking "How do you know how dyslexics feel?" Well it is because I am profoundly dyslexic myself. There are times when I have felt and still feel very isolated in a world that is not dyslexia friendly.

I was five when I first started school, an extremely shy and timid child. I was a very clumsy child with poor concentration and memory and with low self-esteem. Even talking for me was an obstacle. I talked with a slight stammer and would mix up my words, which made everyone laugh and say how stupid I was. My writing was no better. At first, I would write with my left hand, from right to left, everything I wrote was a mirror image. Teachers would hit me on the knuckles with a ruler every time they caught me writing with my left hand. I remember we were made to read aloud in front of the class. I made so many mistakes in the first sentence that I would end up crying with frustration within a few minutes. I found it very difficult to distinguish one word from another. The words were just abstract shapes to me, part of the whole picture. I found that when I did attempt to read, I would say the wrong word or pronounce it incorrectly and would start stuttering. Also, I felt quite ill after concentrating on what I was reading and I would land up with one massive headache, which still happens even now. It is like being on a ship in rough seas trying to read. So attempting to read was not enjoyable and is still not.

I was about six years old, when I was deemed too stupid and lazy to learn anything and was left to my own devices. Throughout my school life, I dreaded going to school, where I was called names and told continually that I was stupid and lazy by everyone. I was constantly bullied, taunted and ridiculed. I lost what little confidence I had in myself and felt as if I was from another planet. I soon learnt how to become invisible and blend into the background, well away from trouble. I became a loner and still find it difficult to mix and talk to people I do not know, though this is improving as I learn to trust people again.

My first job at fifteen was washing dishes in a canteen as I was informed that that was all I was good for. For most of my life, I was dominated by my family and then by my husband. As far as they were concerned, I needed to be told what to do, when to do it and how to do it. They too considered me stupid.

I was forty-seven when I contacted my local further education college, Highlands , for help. I was extremely shy, self-conscious, hesitant and lacked confidence. I did not know how to speak to people or socialise, as a matter of fact; I was absolutely petrified of people. Now I am a totally different person. In the last ten years I have achieved a degree in social science and I support others with learning difficulties.

Why have I told you my story? Because I would like managers to acknowledge that some dyslexics can achieve wonderful things and become successful if only given the chance. For forty-seven years, I thought I was in a world where dyslexic people like me were not wanted or cared about. However, now, ten years later, I know that there are people who do care, who want to understand and support dyslexics. Well, what I want to know is, are you one of these wonderful caring people? If so, please learn about dyslexia and how to you can support dyslexics in your workplace.

So what can be done? In a busy workplace it is not always convenient to help dyslexic employees, but a good starting point is to have an open attitude, patience and most of all understanding. There is plenty of information available through Train to Gain, on the internet, in book and at local Dyslexia Associations that can help with understanding, but one of the best people to ask is the dyslexic employee, they know what works for them.

However, what is really needed is to create a culture of understanding in manages and in business, because with understanding of dyslexia come opportunities for dyslexics to feel able to ask for help. Nevertheless, this can only happen if managers really see the potential of each person, their skills and abilities rather than their dyslexic disabilities. You do not need to become an expert on dyslexia, but by creation a culture of openness and concern you may find that there are employees in your organisation who are held back and who you can help to liberate their potential.

References

Disability Discrimination Act (DDA, 1995/2005), http://www.opsi.gov.uk/acts/acts1995/1995050.htm <https://email2.btconnect.com/exchweb/bin/redir.asp?URL=http://www.opsi.gov.uk/acts/acts1995/1995050.htm> accessed on 10/12/2008 .

Sanderson, Dr. A. (2008), "My Business", www.mybusines.co.uk <https://email2.btconnect.com/exchweb/bin/redir.asp?URL=http://www.mybusines.co.uk/> accessed 10/12/2008

6. Into Employment

6.1 Dyslexia Career Strategies and matching Competencies with Job Requirements

Brian Hagan, Dyslexia Advice and Training for Adults, British Dyslexia Association Organisational Member

1. Is there a 'right' career for a dyslexic person?

Employers often ask me whether certain job families or posts with certain competency requirements are well suited - or not suited - to dyslexic employees. Similarly, people with dyslexia or other specific learning difficulties also frequently seek advice on whether there are particular careers that would suit them, and if there are particular careers that they should avoid at all costs. There is no simple answer to this question, but there are things that both employers and employees can do to avoid mistakes - we outline the most important of these below.

2. Obtaining career advice

In general, career advice for dyslexic adults is sought by three groups of people:

1. Dyslexic adults who are seeking advice on choosing a career which will capitalise on their strengths and motivation, and avoid areas of weakness.

2. Employees who face redundancy or dismissal, or are about to voluntarily leave a job because of performance problems attributable to dyslexia.

3. Employers who want advice on redeploying a dyslexic employee who cannot cope with his/her present job.

This article seeks to provide generic advice that addresses the key question in all their minds - how do we make the best match between the dyslexic employee's competencies profile and the demands of individual jobs and job families?

Firstly the dyslexic adult pondering a future career or career change has to balance a number of factors:

- what career actually inspires them and why;

- what the task/ competency demands of this career are likely to be;

- and whether they feel that, with appropriate support, they will be able to cope reasonably well with those demands.

In practice, people often find themselves in a career 'by accident'. A decision at the age of sixteen about what A-levels to do (perhaps influenced by a desire to avoid 'reading and writing heavy courses' rather than particular interest in a subject) will determine what subjects are later studied at college or University, and ultimately what career is pursued. Once in a job a dyslexic person might realise that the work they are doing does not interest them, or they might like their work but find themselves not fully competent to do it. This competence gap will often be nothing to do with effort or motivation, but more to do with lack of reasonable adjustments and a poor induction process - an argument for disclosure of dyslexia to prospective employers, so that they can ensure appropriate adjustments are made from day one.

It's often hard to decide in advance if a job will be rewarding - and manageable. For a dyslexic person, however, there are some obvious minefields. For example, a person who is a very slow reader might think twice about training as a solicitor or barrister, professions in which large amounts of reading need to be done at short notice. If a person is inaccurate with numbers, perhaps book-keeping is not for them; and if they have poor visual skills, then air traffic controller is probably a poor choice.

There are various ways in which a person can 'try out' a job.

For example, many professional and vocational trainings (e.g., nursing, drama) include practical experience. The government also runs job trialling schemes (see end of article for relevant websites).

When considering career choices, dyslexic people need to be fully aware of their strengths as well as their difficulties, and, if possible, choose a job in which their strengths can be utilised. A person who has literacy difficulties may well have excellent interpersonal, practical or IT skills, or perhaps creative skills and artistic ability. They may have an entrepreneurial flair and be well-suited to being self-employed (preferably with a literate secretary). Vague generalisations about what dyslexic people can and can't do (e.g., 'dyslexic people have good visual skills') are not helpful; each person needs to make a careful appraisal of his/her own strengths and weaknesses.

3. Careers Advice and Matching Competencies with Job Requirements: a Process

Not all careers development is customised for dyslexic people. However, a dyslexia-aware careers development process should work systematically through the following stages:

1. Appraisal.

- Consideration of the individual's general strengths and difficulties, based on self-report and, if available, diagnostic assessment and/or workplace needs reports.

- Consideration of the individual's professional competencies.

2. Overview of the internal or external labour market and training opportunities.

- Review of various occupations and their characteristics/ requirements.

- Advice on reasonable adjustments and training.

- Advice on achieving control at work and in study.

3. Generating options

- Identifying the individual's *niche,* that is, the occupational areas that motivate him/her most.

- Generating options by matching niches to occupational requirements.

- Prioritising options.

- Drawing up an action plan to select appropriate employment or training.

4. Putting the plan into action

- Explaining how to find dyslexia-friendly employers and get further information on specific careers.

- Setting objectives, e.g., making 4 requests each week for job descriptions and person specifications.

- Setting timescales.

- Providing information to support job applications, including preparing an effective CV, discussing issues of disclosure, and practising interview techniques.

- Suggesting resources relevant to the plan, e.g., careers websites, government support, helpful publications.

Bear in mind that this process is generic, and can be readily adapted to HR / Occupational health advice to existing dyslexic employees who are being considered for redeployment or capacity procedures because of 'dyslexia attributable' poor performance in their existing job.

4. **Some successful career choices/changes**

Below are three examples of dyslexic people who were unhappy in their job but who, after taking advice from a dyslexia-aware careers adviser sourced through their HR Department or Trade Union, made a successful career change.

Case 1. Jim was very keen to train as a firefighter, but during his training, questions arose as to whether his dyslexic difficulties, in particular his poor short term memory and slow reaction times, made him unsuitable for this career. Some colleagues felt they could not entirely rely on him in an emergency, and as a result he was subject to a fair amount of bullying. Jim eventually gave up the training course, greatly saddened that he would not be able to pursue his long-held ambition to join the fire service.

Solution: After discussing his situation with an external careers adviser commissioned by his HR department, Jim re-trained as a community safety officer. In this role he was not required to multi task and make on-the-spot decisions without prior warning: he could organise his time and workload in a flexible way. And he had the satisfaction of doing a job he found interesting while offering a vital service to the public.

Case 2. Beatrice's first job was in customer care at a call centre. Here she found it impossible to deal with incoming calls within the very strict time limits demanded by the company and became stressed and depressed. Eventually she was dismissed; her Union argued that her employer should have implemented reasonable adjustments - which in this case might have included career appraisal and internal redeployment or job redesign - and as a result her employer made a significant Out of Court settlement.

Solution: Encouraged by the careers advisor secured by her Trade union, Beatrice looked for a job which utilised her good interpersonal skills, and trained as a Health Care Assistant; she is now very successful in this job. It makes limited demands on literacy, does not depend on quick reaction time, and fully utilises her good people skills.

Case 3. Robert worked as a trainee accountant. Though good with figures, he could not cope with the constant short deadlines and the lack of control over his time and workload. He eventually became depressed and had to leave his job.

Solution. Robert had good IT skills and, on the advice of a careers adviser, he developed these further and set up as a self-employed trainer in assistive technology. He is now very successful in this job which draws on his interests, utilises his strengths and gives him control over work levels and deadlines.

5. Conclusion

- It is vital that before applying for a job, dyslexic candidates should put their strengths and weaknesses in writing in 2 columns, (using their diagnostic assessment where possible).

- Compare these to the job description of the post they wish to apply for, and

- Analyse what proportion of the job requires competencies that they have and have not got.

If they have less than 75% of the key job competencies, and if their potential competency gaps cannot be readily mitigated through reasonable adjustments, then they should avoid the job!

When applying for jobs employers and candidates should remember that the duty to make reasonable adjustments applies to potential as well as existing employees - candidates should be encouraged to make suggestions that will help them display their full range of competencies during the selection process, and employers should be careful to ensure that they do not discriminate against potential dyslexic employees by using methods which treat them less favourably than non-dyslexic candidates.

In general terms employers should:

- Assess only the knowledge, skills and experience required for the effective performance of the job;

- Do so in ways which are as close to the circumstances of that job and its performance as possible;

- Ensure that the panel has an understanding of dyslexia based on the information in this publication, and understand how dyslexia might affect a candidate's interview performance.

For example, it would be reasonable for an employer to waive written tests if writing were not a significant part of the job applied for. Dyslexic candidates could be allowed more time to complete such tests.

Instructions for manual tests could be clearly read aloud to the candidate or audibly-recorded to avoid dyslexic candidates being penalised due to problems with short-term memory.

My experience in human resources and as a Consultant and tutor advising dyslexic students/ candidates for employment, employees and their employers, has shown me that there has been a great deal of progress in promoting awareness of dyslexia in the workplace. However, it is still early days in translating this awareness into policies and processes which help avoid career selection mistakes, and improve the match between a dyslexic candidate's/ employee's competencies and the job requirements. I am happy to correspond with employers and employees who would like to further these goals.

Brian Hagan

Before moving into specialist dyslexia consultancy and tuition in 2001, Brian worked at Head of Professional Function Level in Human Resources and Training, where his responsibilities included Recruitment, Selection, Appraisal and Career Development for 1600 multidisciplinary staff.

Over the past two years he has been increasingly involved in providing customised careers advice and support to dyslexic employees.

Brian may be contacted for careers advice on

- <u>bhdyslexia@yahoo.co.uk</u> or
- By phone on 020 8348 7110.

6.2 How SKIDZ Supports the Dyslexic Individual

Steve Godfrey

Introduction to SKIDZ

SKIDZ Motor Projects provide practical learning opportunities for young people, many of them experiencing difficulties with mainstream schooling. We provide these courses in well equipped workshops mainly in the Thames Valley but also working with other projects across the country. The High Wycombe project has just celebrated its tenth anniversary and now works with approximately 350 young people a week. The main age range is thirteen to sixteen but if younger or older need our services we will take them if possible. The students come from a wide range of backgrounds and have many different difficulties but the common theme is that they do not like school.

The courses we offer include re-engagement, entry level and level 1 as well as purely recreational ones where people come in their own time to learn more about their vehicles. Our aim is to give them the chance to continue their education or to secure gainful employment.

The Staff

Our instructors have a wealth of experience in vehicle maintenance and repair and a passion for working with young people who want to learn but struggle with the usual teaching methods offered. Few of the instructors have nationally recognized teaching qualifications but their ability to successfully convey information to the students in a way they can understand and retain is often commented on in a very positive way.

We have dyslexic members of staff and their understanding of the problems some of our students experience helps us to ensure we can support them in their learning. When new information sheets, test papers and other fact sheets are developed all of the staff are involved to make sure they are useable by everyone.

We provide specific training about learning difficulties, dyslexia and other problems for all our staff. This is provided by the Wycombe Pupil Referral Unit who we work closely with and we have many of their students on our courses. This is the only senior PRU to have been judged as outstanding by Ofsted twice running and works hard at early intervention rather than as a place of last resort for young people unable or unwilling to fit into the mainstream school system.

The Students

A common misconception is that young people who misbehave at school and cause disruption in the classroom are doing it because they do not want to learn or cannot learn. When these same young people come to SKIDZ they are nearly always polite, well mannered and very keen to learn. How can they be so different in the two environments?

At junior school they are assessed purely on reading and writing abilities and if they are poor at these then they know they are seen as failing and their self esteem drops. In many cases of course there are reasons behind their lack of literacy skills, which can include dyslexia, but in many cases these are not discovered and they do not improve. In upper schools learning is mainly through reading and understanding is demonstrated mainly by writing. If you are already poor at these what chance do you have? Boredom and disillusion set in, you are often being told off and in many cases bad behaviour follows often followed by exclusion. There are of course schools that do not work this way but far too many do.

At SKIDZ learning is by doing, assessment is by practical, verbal and other methods and suddenly the young people start achieving and they like it. As soon as they like it they want more, their behaviour improves and in over ninety percent of cases the young people leave at sixteen and continue into employment, education or training.

We have many case studies showing the successes of our students including one where the young person had always been in trouble at his schools and was eventually excluded. After being a model student at SKIDZ for two years he secured an apprenticeship and when he started at college they assessed him as dyslexic and provided him with the support he needed to complete his course.

Supporting the Dyslexic

Supporting the dyslexic students and instructors is not very different to supporting everyone else as long as you believe that everyone is an individual and cater for their needs accordingly. Many people speak louder to people in wheelchairs as if not having the use of their legs makes them deaf. In the same way people seem to believe that people who have problems reading and writing are not clever but experience shows us the opposite is often the case.

There is a lot of information available to help organisations and individuals to support dyslexics in the workplace, see the BDA website for example, but one of the simplest things to do is ask them and listen to what they say.

What comes out of those discussions will be different for each individual but may include providing voice recognition on laptops so that if you prefer written reports to be sent to you this can be done without taking your dyslexic employee hours at home. Maybe the colours you use in spreadsheets could be changed to make it easier for dyslexics to read, maybe your recruitment methods need to be looked at to see if they prejudice dyslexics.

Do you offer different ways of learning to your employees? Do you use the way dyslexics often look at problems in a different way to benefit your organisation or are their views seen as too weird to be considered?

All you need to do is look at the famous successful dyslexics and you will see that if you do not support, develop and encourage the dyslexics in your organisation you will not benefit fully from their talents.

6.3 Dyslexia in the Workplace: the Legal Requirements

John Mackenzie, Trustee, British Dyslexia Association

The Disability Discrimination Act 2005 (the DDA) makes an employer liable to pay compensation for discrimination to a disabled person, either an employee, a contract worker or as a job applicant (all referred to as 'employee' in this article).

A disabled person is defined by the DDA as one who has a long standing condition that has an adverse effect on his or her ability to perform day-to-day tasks. As dyslexia is a life-long condition, provided it is sufficiently serious, an employee with dyslexic difficulties is disabled under the Act.

The condition needs only to be 'more than trivial' to be disabling. In practice where a dyslexic candidate is considered to be in need of 25% extra time in tests and exams (an almost standard recommendation in assessment reports that diagnose dyslexia) the individual will be disabled under the Act.

Actions on the part of the employer that can give rise to liability are:

- failure to appoint to a position,

- failure to promote,

- dismissing or causing *'any other detriment'*.

Discrimination can be caused by:

- direct discrimination,

- indirect discrimination (or disability related discrimination),

- harassment,

- victimisation,

- a failure to make reasonable adjustments.

These can be characterised in the following examples:

- "You are sacked because you are dyslexic" = direct discrimination.

- "You are sacked because you are slow in reacting to instructions" (due to dyslexia) = indirect or disability related discrimination.

- "Because you are slow in reacting to instructions, I am going to punch you on the nose" = harassment.

- "Because you are taking me to the employment tribunal for punching you on the nose, you are sacked" = victimisation.

Reasonable Adjustments

Dyslexia is often not easily recognised either by the employee with dyslexic difficulties or the employer. Dyslexic adults often develop coping strategies that may conceal the underlying disability from others. Many dyslexic adults are unaware that they are dyslexic.

It is not a legal requirement to disclose dyslexic difficulties, and it is not always necessary for the employer to know that the employee is disabled. However, where there are disability related problems relating to performance, failure to implement reasonable adjustments becomes a discrimination issue.

The obligation to implement reasonable adjustments for an employee arises when an employer's system, categorised in the DDA as a 'provision, criterion or practice', places the dyslexic employee at a substantial disadvantage in comparison with persons who are not dyslexic. It is then the duty of the employer to institute reasonable adjustments to prevent the system having that effect.

To establish discrimination through failure to implement reasonable adjustments, it is necessary to prove that the employer knew or ought to have known that the person is disabled and in need of the adjustments.

An employer, particularly in a large and sophisticated organisation, will increasingly be expected to pick up the signs that an employee may be dyslexic, even if the employee is not aware of the condition.

If a tribunal finds that objectively a particular adjustment should have been implemented it will not matter that the employer was unaware of the adjustment: there will have been a breach of the DDA.

Identifying Reasonable Adjustments

What steps should an employer take to ensure that the organisation complies with the DDA in respect of reasonable adjustments?

The first and essential step is to ensure that all key staff, including in particular line managers, Occupational Health and Human Resources staff are trained in the effects of dyslexia and how it may be identified in an employee.

In an individual case, where an employee has declared himself/ herself to be dyslexic, or it is suspected that the employee may be dyslexic, the employer must ensure that he has prompt access to a full professional assessment of the employee's condition. If no historic assessment is available from the employee, an assessment will have to be commissioned. There are many expert chartered psychologists across the country, and organisations such as the British Dyslexia Association that will assist in identifying a suitable expert. It should take no longer than a month for the assessment to be carried out and the report provided to the employer and the employee.

Once the employee is identified as dyslexic and the assessment has identified the areas of strengths and weaknesses, line managers, OH and HR need to be fully briefed so that accommodation of the employee's dyslexia can begin without delay.

The next essential stage is to commission a workplace needs assessment to determine what adjustments are required to compensate for the employee's dyslexia. The employee can be encouraged to make an application to Access to Work, the JobCentre Plus department that looks after the interests of disabled workers. Access to Work will conduct a free workplace assessment, advise on the adjustments required and provide a substantial proportion of the cost of the adjustments from government funds.

The Access to Work report will constitute compelling evidence for an employment tribunal of the adjustments that the employer should implement or should have implemented, so that it is essential that the employer moves swiftly to implement the adjustments recommended.

These may include:

- Dyslexia awareness training for the employer's staff,
- Specific dyslexia related coaching or training for the employee,

- Technological aids such as voice to text and text to voice computer software, a digital recorder to record information and instructions, headphones for the software, mind mapping software, special spell checks and other equipment.

- Adjustments to working practices and the working environment.

It may be necessary to change the employee's responsibilities or provide additional training. It may in some cases be necessary to offer the employee a transfer to other duties. The DDA sets out a list of areas of adjustment that may be appropriate.

Legal Implications

In employment tribunal claims brought by dyslexic employees, the failure to implement reasonable adjustments can be a significant aspect. Often failures arise because no one seems to have had the responsibility to implement the adjustments once identified.

There are two further features of cases brought under the DDA that are particularly significant:

- The first is the shifting burden of proof: if the employee establishes that there have been circumstances which might, if unexplained, amount to actionable discrimination, the onus falls on the employer to prove that the circumstances were not actionable discrimination.

■ The second consideration, and an important one, is that there is no cap on the compensation that an employment tribunal may award a claimant under the DDA. If, for example, a dyslexic apprentice is dismissed because he failed an exam which, with reasonable adjustments, he would have passed, the employer may have to compensate the ex-apprentice for the loss of an entire career in that field.

John Mackenzie
Employment Law Solicitor

6.4 Case Study

Peter Hall, Professional Photographer

I was fortunate to have my dyslexia spotted when I was eight years old thus receiving the help that I needed from an early age. Throughout my education I suffered by not doing well in exams and tests, whether that was because of my dyslexia I don't really know.

However, a breakthough came at university when I was studying for my Product Design degree. In my first year I tried to work in the same fashion as the other students but with little success. Then one day, a third year student gave me some advice. He simply said to me that if I wanted my work to improve, stand out and be noticed, then I had to do it in my own way from the initial idea to the final presentation. Taking this basic concept not only did I feel more confident in what I was designing but I also produced better work.

After university I tried different jobs and careers and eventually tried photography, for which I had always had a passion and interest.

I managed to build up a bit of a portfolio in the classic car world and in doing so slowly taught myself the art of car photography. I got a few lucky breaks with some truly amazing cars but after a while I wanted to turn what I had learnt with classic cars to motor racing, with the view of putting my own artistic slant on it.

I have built a portfolio of racing photography, cars from the Le Mans series, FIA GT, Formula 1 and Goodwood classic racers.

This has enabled me to hold my own exhibition of photography on Ferraris and write a couple of car photography coffee table books.

It has taken time and a lot of effort and I still have a lot of goals that I want to reach within photography. I want to continue exploring new ideas and avenues of work but I have learnt to accept that I have certain weaknesses, namely spelling, writing and especially anything to do with numbers. I have, therefore, focused on my strengths of creativity and the ability to think 'outside of the box'. Moreover, I have learnt never to accept 'that things can't be done' and that there is always another way of approaching things.

6.5 Legal Remedies

Melanie Jameson, Dyslexia Consultancy, Malvern

This handbook charts the successes and challenges faced by people with dyslexia and related conditions in the workplace. I shall focus on the challenges, tracing the pathway from difficulties in employment to the decision to seek legal remedies. Various outcomes will be illustrated by case studies and good practice will be highlighted.

My early experiences of observing the workplace problems of adults with dyslexia occurred during many years of facilitating Lancaster Adult Dyslexics. One by one our committee succumbed to the effects of trying to operate in a hostile environment. G, a postman, was denied the reasonable adjustments that would enable him to take promotional exams. He was subject to ever-changing demands as his round was increased and varied at short notice and the sorting system was revamped.

J, working in the local Benefits Office, also faced the dyslexic employee's greatest challenge - a new system. He now had to see far more clients per session and do the paperwork at the end of the day. He could not keep up and became more and more stressed until he had to take time off work.

L, employed in Career Guidance, was bullied, in small ways at first, because she did not operate in quite the same way as her colleagues. In an over-worked department, where employee stress levels were high, her line manger picked on someone who was different and made her life a misery. She started to suffer from psychosomatic symptoms but received little support from her GP. Determined not to be browbeaten, L started on the long route of holding her employers to account for forcing a constructive dismissal and acting in a discriminatory fashion.

Thus Lancaster Adult Dyslexics gradually closed down, as key members became incapacitated due to a combination of factors:

■ lack of appreciation of the need for dyslexic employees to reach established gaols by their own routes.

■ failure to apply *Reasonable Adjustments* as laid out in the Disability Discrimination Act (DDA)

■ an unwillingness , on the part of employers, to sort out problem areas early on, before things escalated into a full-blown dispute or stress-related illness.

The involvement of Occupational Health seldom seemed to resolve these issues since dyslexia was rarely understood and difficulties were attributed to mental health problems.

So what are the Legal Remedies?

The most useful piece of legislation is still the Disability Discrimination Act (1995 onwards) which addresses the area of employment by outlining the areas in which the impact of a disability should be accommodated and establishing that the undermining of coping strategies also counts as discrimination - the example given even refers to dyslexia:

In some cases people have 'coping strategies' which cease to work in some circumstances (for example, where someone who stutters or has dyslexia is placed under stress).

The principle of *Reasonable Adjustments* is emphasised as the way forward; in my experience this approach is most successful where the employee has a clear view of his workplace needs and how these can be best addressed. In the case of J in the Benefits Office, we met to clarify the issues and decided the best way forward was to compose a letter to his Line Manager pairing each of his difficulties with 'reasonable' solutions. The Disability Discrimination Act was referred to, together with J's membership of a national dyslexia charity, the overall tone being:

'Let's sort this out amicably so there is no need to put things on a formal footing'.

It worked - J's issues were taken into consideration and no further steps were needed.

The Disability Equality Duty (1996), which many organisations are now obliged to sign up to, is a less satisfactory piece of legislation to support individual claims. In my experience, internal and external consultations with people with disabilities are not reflected in the resulting Disability Equality Scheme which is usually phrased in very general terms. Although the resulting Impact Assessments sometimes seem more like box-ticking exercises, the consideration of disability issues and the move towards a cross-departmental 'whole organisation approach' should be beneficial. Employees with dyslexia who wish to change things in their organisations should consider putting themselves forward for internal disability committees, thus contributing to changing the culture. If they feel they are facing discrimination it is worth looking at their organisation's Disability Equality Scheme to see if the document provides them with useful back-up.

Only if other paths have been exhausted should an employee with dyslexia consider having recourse to an Employment Tribunal; having your competence probed and areas of weakness exposed is bound to be a distressing experience, aggravated by the protracted nature of some hearings. In cases of dismissal, disciplinary action or employee grievance the emphasis is on trying to resolve the issues through Dispute Resolution Procedures (2004) whereby documentation passes between employee and employer, within given time limits. However, coping with the documentation can be very daunting for adults with information processing difficulties.

The following case study highlights the difficulties encountered by a dyslexic employee in the preparation of her case.

I have worked as a hairdresser for many years but have only recently been diagnosed as dyslexic. Following a whiplash injury, I asked my employer if I could work on a high stool rather than standing, but he said I couldn't. In fact I'd have to leave the job if I could not stand up like the others. I thought this was 'unfair dismissal' and after struggling on for a time decided to take him to an employment tribunal. I found a solicitor and was told I'd have to have more medical examinations.

This is when my problems really started: no-one explained the legal procedures properly. I tried - and failed - to make my solicitor and the medical specialists aware of how my dyslexia affects me, but found them very unsympathetic. They seemed to feel that I was using my dyslexia as an excuse and mentioned successful celebrity dyslexics, such as Duncan Goodhew or Richard Branson, pointing out how well they've done. The suggestion seemed to be that I am a failure. I kept feeling I was not giving a clear enough account of the events leading up to my unfair dismissal claim, and their impact on my life. I found the whole process both exhausting and dispiriting.

At the last minute she withdrew, giving her reasons, as follows:

My confidence in the whole process, and in particular in the individuals involved, has disintegrated. I am very concerned

JUSTMENTS DOCUMENTATION SHOULD

ummary of the situation and list of reports
ents undertaken.

f the individual's dyslexic / dyspraxic /
difficulties.

idations for *Reasonable Adjustments*, arising
iblished difficulties, as illustrated by the
examples:

e rather than *compound / multi-clausal*
s.

X to check understanding by rephrasing
is without censure or (implied) criticism (as
iry).

vorking memory difficulties into account and
X sufficient time to check back with his/her
, especially when reporting particular dates and
ences of actions

e allowances if X has difficulty answering concisely.

w X to take a ten minute break after every hour of
ceedings (as necessary) to restore concentration.

rences

e *Employment Act 2002 (Dispute Resolution) Regulations
004)*

ie *Disability Discrimination Act (2005)*

slexia in the workplace - A Guide for Unions B Hagan
005) TUC Publications

dult *Dyslexia: Awareness & Good Practice for Employers M*

Dyslexia Vocational Evaluation Service

Remploy has developed a unique service
identifying individual dyslexia traits which
can then be used to recommend reasonable
adjustments at work. They can also be used
to identify most suited job goals and remove
or reduce barriers to work.

The service provides a vocational approach
for employers, employees and job seekers and
can identify if a full psychological assessment is
needed resulting in improved performance,
confidence and self esteem.

For information, or
a quotation call us on
0845 146 0501
www.remploy.co.uk

Remploy
Putting ability first

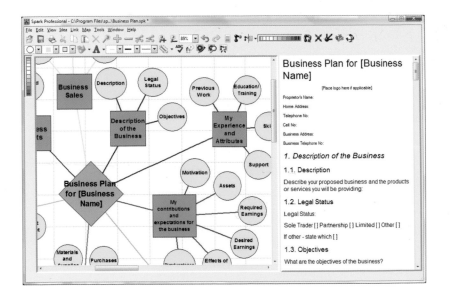
that I will not be
the forthcoming
grasp what the qu
myself down.

L, from Career Guid
and had her claim up
success is documentati
individual's Specific Lea
should be taken to accom
DDA model of Reasonable
The Tribunal Chair, who is
be directed to the Equal Trea
contains a section on Specific
updated definitions of the conc
helpful if the employee's represe
Official, is well informed; a usefu
Sheet: Dyslexia in the workplace -

If good practice is followed, there is
remedies should not be successful in
discrimination.

252 Employment and D

REASONABLE AD
CONTAIN:

1. A very brief s
   and assessm

2. An outline
   attentional

3. Recommer
   out of est
   following

- Ask singl
  question

- Enable
  questio
  necess

- Take
  allow
  notes
  sequ

- Mak

- All
  pr

Refe

Th
(2

Jameson (2005) Lancaster Adult Dyslexics

Better Dispute Resolution: A Review of Employment Dispute Resolution in Great Britain M Gibbons (2007) DTI

*Equal Treatment Bench Book Sections 5.5 and 5.6 (2008 revision) Judicial Studies Board

*available from M Jameson, email: dyslexia.mj@dsl.pipex.com

6.6 Preparing Students for Employment

Barry Hayward

Dyslexia is a syndrome that includes a combination of both strengths and weaknesses. It is established by a series of tests that highlight discrepancies between a person's general level of intelligence and abilities in aspects of literacy and sometimes numeracy.

Significant weaknesses may be identified in short-term and working memory, speed of processing, sequencing skills, auditory and/or visual perception, spoken language and motor skills. Abilities can include, imaginative and creative thinking, intuitive understanding and determination.

Put simply a dyslexic person may take longer to process information, but can otherwise reach the same standard of work as any other employee.

Dyslexic students (provided they declare their disability) receive a high level of support at university. This will include some or all of the following:

- Provision to record lectures.

- Tutors and markers are informed of the student's dyslexia so it is taken into account when assessing work.

- Additional time in examinations.

- Software to assist with planning and structuring work and spelling etc.

- Specialist tutoring from a dyslexia tutor to develop learning strategies.

On entering employment a graduate may require similar levels of provision in order to reach the potential they are capable of.

Supporting Dyslexic Employees

Some examples of the difficulties that may arise in work include:

Retention of verbal instructions due to short term memory difficulties: as soon as it is heard it is forgotten. Making notes is helpful, but dyslexics often find taking notes difficult. Giving instructions in writing as well as verbally is helpful.

Difficulty retaining information read: so may need to read same thing several times, resulting in slower reading e.g. reports, emails etc. Providing key points or summaries is helpful. Be prepared for the employee to need more time.

Organisational skills: Use of diary systems and simply remembering dates and so on are often a problem for dyslexic employees. Providing additional guidance or training in planning, time management, office systems would be helpful.

Writing: Poor spelling, grammar, punctuation and handwriting is commonly a feature of dyslexia. If the employee is required to produce reports, documents or other written guidance, then software support and possibly colleague support will be needed.

Key Strategies to Maximise Performance.

Firstly be understanding and supportive. Provide the opportunity to discuss difficulties. Positive communication is likely to reassure the employee and lead to the employee providing solutions.

Explore technology that may help. Start by contacting the British Dyslexia Association: www.bdadyslexia.org.uk.

Allow the employee opportunities to prepare. This can be done by providing as much information in advance of meetings as possible. Taking the time to talk through documents is also a positive approach.

More details of reasonable adjustments can found at:

www.bdadyslexia.org.uk/adjustments.

Identifying Dyslexia in Employees

Dyslexic employees (and job applicants) may not declare a disability when applying for employment. Firstly they may not view dyslexia as a disability.

It is a very positive step to encourage employees and applicants to declare dyslexia. Perhaps use the phrase "declare a disability (this includes dyslexia)".

Graduates who have received support whilst at university will have documentary evidence of their dyslexia. It is reasonable to expect such evidence from employees.

You may suspect an employee has dyslexia, but the employee may not have been tested. Dyslexia is identified by a series of tests carried out by a Chartered Psychologist specialising in adult dyslexia.

Having an assessment done will help you and the employee to establish what reasonable adjustments can help.

Recruitment

Dyslexic students / graduates can be disadvantaged in the recruitment process depending on the approaches taken.

Online application forms can be problematic as dyslexics often like to work on drafts many times over. Being logged on to a recruitment site for a long period isn't always practical. Downloads of application forms in a Word format are preferable.

Interviews are opportunities for dyslexics to shine as verbal skills are often a strength. However answers may be affected by short term memory issues. Being understanding of this and allowing interviewees time to think through before answering is helpful.

Recruitment Tests: A prospective applicant declaring dyslexia should be offered additional time to complete any tests.

25% additional time is the standard offered in tests and exams.

Specialist Employment Guidance

For graduates looking for work or employers seeking to widen their recruitment pool there are a number of agencies working with disabled / dyslexic graduates seeking employment. These include:

University of London Careers Group:
www.careers.lon.ac.uk/output/page111

Employment Opportunities for people with disabilities:
http://www.opportunities.org.uk/Page.aspx?page=2380BAB4-AA95-4609-BC64-E6EE7A6E4DDE
Email: sarah.scadding@eopps.org
Tel: 0207 448 5442

Scope - Leadership Recruitment Scheme:
www.scope.org.uk/graduates
Email : graduates@scope.org.uk
Tel. 020 7619 7299
Minicom 020 7619 7187

EmployAbility
www.employ-ability.org.uk
Tel: 07852 764 684
Email: info@eability.org

Disability Discrimination Act (2005):

The Disability Discrimination Act describes a disability as:
"a physical or mental impairment which has a substantial
and long-term adverse effect on a person's ability to carry out
normal day-to-day activities".

'Long term' is usually considered to be a year or more. For a
fuller definition, please see the government web site:
http://www.direct.gov.uk/en/DisabledPeople/
RightsAndObligations/DisabilityRights/DG_4001069

Paterson v The Commissioner of Police of the Metropolis [2007]

In this case, it was established that for dyslexia to fit the
definition of disability defined in the Act, the difficulties do not
have to be severe.

His case concerned his contention that his employer failed to
make reasonable adjustments during promotion exams. The Act
talks about disability having an impact on everyday activities.
Whilst it was argued that promotional examinations are not
everyday activities the Employment Appeal Tribunal (EAT) held
that they were not in any way unusual and so can be deemed to
be normal day-to-day activities.

The EAT's view was that carrying out an assessment or
examination is a normal day-to-day activity. Normal activities
must encompass the activities that are relevant to participation
in professional life.

The EAT said that when assessing the effect of a disability, the comparison is not with the population at large, but with the way in which the individual would carry out the activity if not impaired.

Mr Paterson's dyslexia was described as mild, but it was found to have substantial affects in comparison to other applicants for the role. Therefore the work undertaken is relevant as well as the general affects of the disability.

6.7 Retailing and Dyslexia

Trevor Hobbs, Trustee, British Dyslexia Association

Much of what is discussed in this book is about the dyslexic employee. We must also consider the chances of the purchaser of your product being dyslexic. Every tenth person who enters your salesroom has some level of dyslexia. Don't dismiss this article on the grounds that your customers are intelligent people who couldn't possibly suffer from any form of learning disability. Many of the world's richest and most dynamic people are dyslexic and you are not to know who they are standing at the counter.

Many highly skilled tradesmen are very clever with their hands and can hold very intellectual conversations on a vast range of subjects, but still struggle with poor short term memory and poor written skills.

There is no visual way of identifying the dyslexic customer. The first sign may come when you ask the customer to fill in a form or questionnaire, suddenly they become distressed sometimes to the point that they may just walk away from the sale or refuse to complete the paperwork. Sales agreements for some reason, best known to the compiler are often produced on dark coloured paper with small black printing. Studying this is not a pleasure for anybody to read. The dyslexia standard is clear typeface on buff paper using the Plain English Society guidelines. Just give the person time to digest the content. Dyslexic people are easily distracted by events around them like flashing signs or sudden noise and may need to read over it a couple of times. It's not helped by an impatient salesperson hurrying to close the deal.

Dyslexic people may have a lower credit rating than you would expect just because if they can't fill in the forms correctly or just forget what day a payment is due and they fall behind briefly.

I have heard bank staff refuse to allow customers to take a form home to complete, and dyslexic adults frightened to ask for help in the bank to read the form. They may require the help of a partner either as a reader or scribe. Much distress can be caused by so called 'company policy' where staff have refused to help fill in a customer's application form.

The computer shop where the person was told: just read the instructions; it's easy to follow. Not if you are in your forties and have a reading age of an eight year old, and there are thousands of customers with that sort of reading age.

The counter staff commenting to one another on who wears the trousers in that house "she filled in all the paperwork and he just scribbled his signature". This may well have been a classic case of dyslexia, when he relies on help from his partner to do the written work but he uses his skills to produce a good income for the benefit of both of them. This management of skills is not to be mocked by somebody who found learning the basics at school easy.

Many people struggle with self-assembly furniture but often dyslexic people find this task easy as the instructions are mainly based on a series of drawing. The little bit of written instructions may say 'screw and glue' and if the glue is not there it will be put together without because the dyslexic person has only studied the pictures: to understand a diagram is easier to understand than words. But that's the way the dyslexic brain functions best: in pictorial form. Straight lines of nondescript repeating symbols mean little. That's writing, and it's not the easiest way a dyslexic understands instructions.

Often product instructions are written by one of the manufacturer's techno boffins using a language only somebody who has worked in that industry for years would readily understand. This is a struggle for anybody new to a product and often impossible for the dyslexic individual to comprehend and apply in the correct order. The use of abbreviations is very confusing and means you need to stop reading while thinking of the full meaning of that term. Many companies just expect the customer to know what the abbreviation means without ever using the full meaning. Please use the Plain English Guide when writing instructions and present them in a readable size typeface.

Before the dyslexic shopper even gets to your store they have already had to contend with a number of often stressful situations. The most severely dyslexic adults don't drive a car. This is due to coordination more than literacy problems, but they still need to get on the right bus to get to the shopping centre. If they live in a place with a single bus service it's not much of a problem as long as they remember which side of the road to stand. In towns where a multitude of buses use the same stop they have to remember the number and the words next to them in a short space of time as the bus approaches them. They may have to remember the 56 goes to town but the 65 goes to town station which is a mile from the shops. This can be very confusing for the severely dyslexic individual.

The milder dyslexic individual will drive but probably forget where they left the car in the multi-storey car park and what the registration number is, while in a state of panic. Once in the shop the customer may ask for directions to a particular counter. The shop assistant, being helpful, gives all the directions one could ever need but sadly the dyslexic customer has forgotten most of them before the assistant has finished speaking, and is seen endlessly wandering around the store asking for directions and only being able to remember a part each time. The other situation in stores is "well it was here last time I came in the store": moving stock around the store is little help to the customer, especially that valued 10% who are dyslexic. We navigate by landmarks not by reading notice boards.

Presentation of products has been known to cause confusion. Quoting a couple of cases I have been involved with: the first is an own brand tin of tomatoes, one is whole tomatoes the other is chopped tomatoes, both have the same picture of tomatoes on the label but one tin says whole and the other chopped. This can cause any shopper in a hurry a brief problem, but the severely dyslexic shopper will rely on the picture for product guidance.

Now a much more worrying case was the severely dyslexic person (and that's around 4% of the population) who was found to have tins of dog meat in the store cupboard and didn't own a dog. They had brought it as tinned stewing beef, because that's what the picture on the label resembled. Writing in small print on the label stating

"This product is not fit for human consumption" is no help to a person who can't read.

Some dyslexic people find it very hard to write their own name in any way that is readable. They know their writing is in a style of a very young child and feel very embarrassed by it and will go to great lengths not to ever apply pen to paper. The person with the dog food was in fact a brilliant musician who had travelled the world playing and writing music for a living.

They wrote the music in their own understandable patterns then played it to somebody who could turn it into the accepted format. Travelling as a band the dyslexic musician always had friends around to help. At home alone, they were a very frightened person who really was disabled in our literacy driven society.

Thankfully most dyslexic people manage in our society with a little understanding from the rest of the community. I know many dyslexic adults who will only see one person in the bank or post office because that person understands their problem and helps with the paperwork and if that person is not on duty they will walk out, sometimes at great personal cost.

Busy noisy environments tend not to be dyslexia-friendly places. The age of the moving information screen is problematic: we need the letter to stay still; for your eyes to have to move endlessly across the screen is not helpful at all. We only ever get half the message and we have probably got it wrong anyway.

Remembering a vast number of passwords is normally an impossible task even once we have learnt them we confuse one set with another or enter them backwards.

The person who tries to give a telephone number at breakneck speed is no help to a dyslexic who will never manage to write it down correctly at that speed, hence they never call back and your company has lost a sale.

Clear labelling and instructions are a benefit to everybody.

Techno jargon impresses few people and often loses more sales than it generates. The pace in any form of selling needs to slow down a little and accept that not everybody can consume knowledge at the rapid rate of an expert in the subject.

We are moving into an ageing population and older people like dyslexic people absorb information just that bit slower than society expects to us to do.

All we ask is a bit of understanding and patience: just because you can't see a problem that does not mean there isn't a little problem hidden away.

Trevor Hobbs

BDA Trustee

Adult Dyslexia Access

Index of Advertisers

Adult Dyslexia Access .... Divider

Adult Dyslexia Centre (Thames Valley) .... Divider

BDA .... Back Cover

Claro Software ....**x**

Continuum Books .... Divider

Do-IT Solutions .... Divider

Dyslexia Assessment & Consultancy 212

Dyslexia Solutions 244

Efalex .... Divider

Iansyst .... Inside Front Cover

Independent Dyslexia Consultants 246

Lucem Ltd 24

Lucid .... Divider

Nuance Communications .... Divider

Olympus DS-65 .... Divider

Pico Education .... Divider

Remploy .... Divider

Right to Write .... Inside Back Cover

Shapwick School ....**x**

Spark Space .... Divider

Text and Teach Systems 110

Texthelp Systems .... Divider

Trovus .... Divider

Wiley-Blackwell 225

Words Worldwide Ltd 134